Portrait of the
CANADIAN ROCKIES

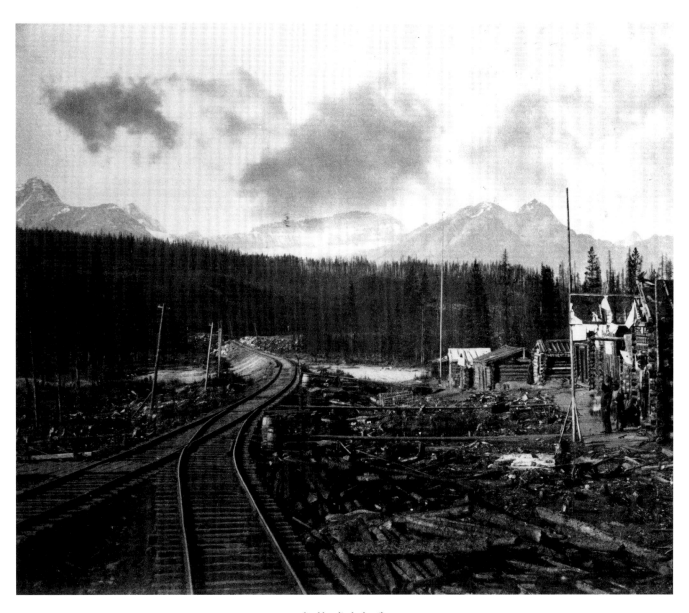

Edited by Elizabeth Wilson

RMB

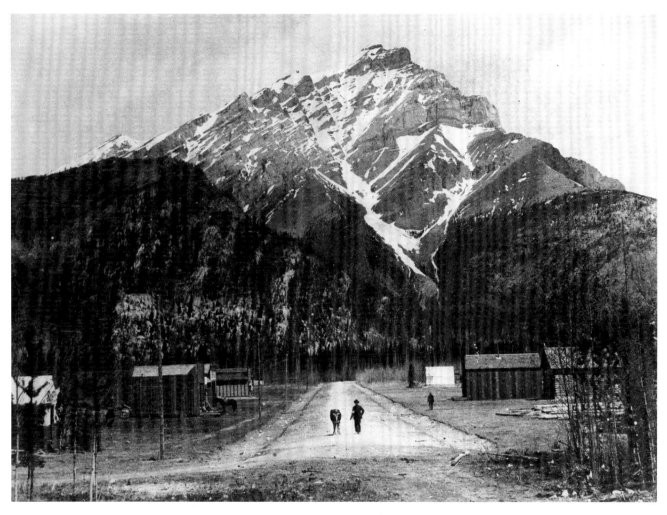

Previous page:
Laggan (Lake Louise)
An early view of the town of Laggan, later renamed Lake Louise.
photo ca.1885

Above:
Cascade Mountain and Banff Avenue
This famous photo shows Banff Avenue in 1887.

Front cover:
The Wenkchemna Peaks
A sea of peaks stretches to the horizon near Moraine Lake in Banff nartional Park.
Photo by Douglas Leighton

Back Cover:
Angel Glacier
this glacier hangs from the side of Mt.Edith Cavell.
Photo by Lee Simmons

Photos by Michel Ball, Van Christou, J.C. Dunlop, Carole Harmon, Don Harmon, Stephen Hutchings, Douglas Leighton, Ian Martin, Scott Rowed, R.W. Sandford, Joe Scanlon, Dennis Schmidt, Lee Simmons

Text© Elizabeth Wilson 2013

Rocky Mountain Books
www.rmbooks.com

Rocky Mountain Books acknowledges the financial support for its publishing program from the Government of Canada through the Canada Book Fund (CBF) and the Canada Council for the Arts, and from the province of British Columbia through the British Columbia Arts Council and the Book Publishing Tax Credit.

Library and Archives Canada Cataloguing in Publication

Portrait of the Canadian Rockies / edited by Elizabeth Wilson.

Previously published under title: Canadian Rockies.
ISBN 978-1-897522-19-6 (bound).—ISBN 978-1-897522-18-9 (pbk.)

1. Rocky Mountains, Canadian (B.C. and Alta.)—Pictorial works. 2. Rocky Mountains, Canadian (B.C. and Alta.)—History—Pictorial works. I. Wilson, Elizabeth, 1961-

FC219.P66 2008   971.10022'2   C2008-905866-6

Printed and bound in Canada.

This book was produced using FSC®-certified, acid-free paper, processed chlorine free and printed with vegetable-based inks.

 Canadian Heritage Patrimoine canadien

 Canada Council for the Arts   Conseil des Arts du Canada

 BRITISH COLUMBIA ARTS COUNCIL

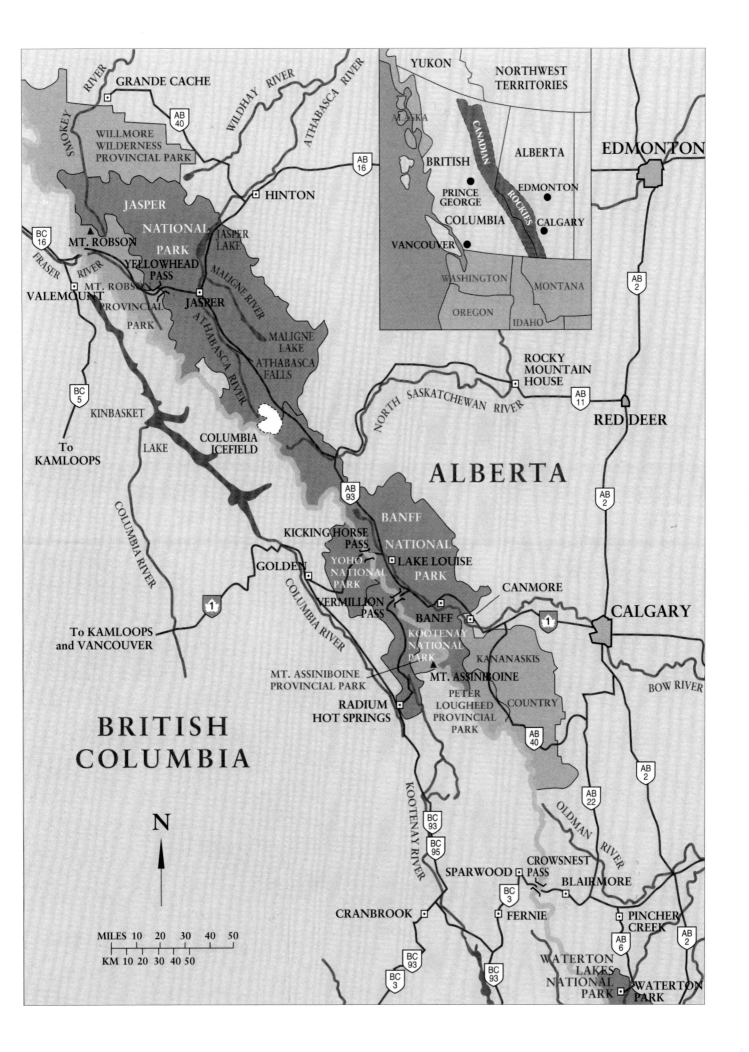

Top:
The Banff train station
Lined up and waiting for a train, these passengers stand in front of the log structure that served as an early station house and ticket office.
photo ca.1900

Bottom:
RCMP and Bow Falls
As famous as Canada itself, the Royal Canadian Mounted Police with their brilliant scarlet jackets and round-brimmed hats, were the symbol of order and control in the early days in Canada's rugged west.

Opposite:
Mt. Assiniboine
The "Matterhorn of the Rockies," Mt Assiniboine's distinctive triangular shape is artfully mimicked by the teepee pitched in the meadow at its base.

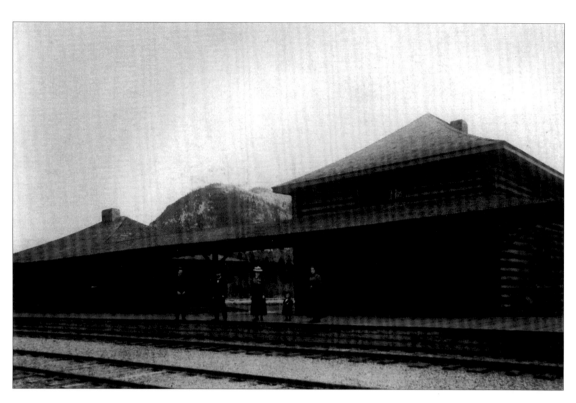

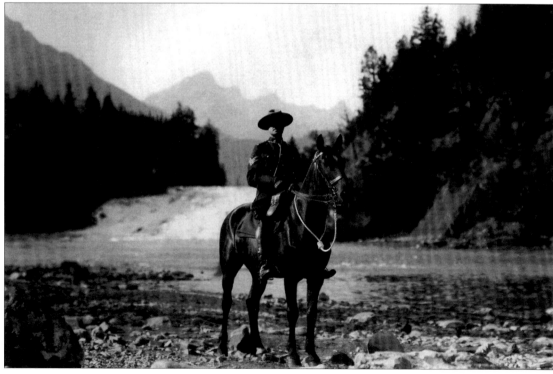

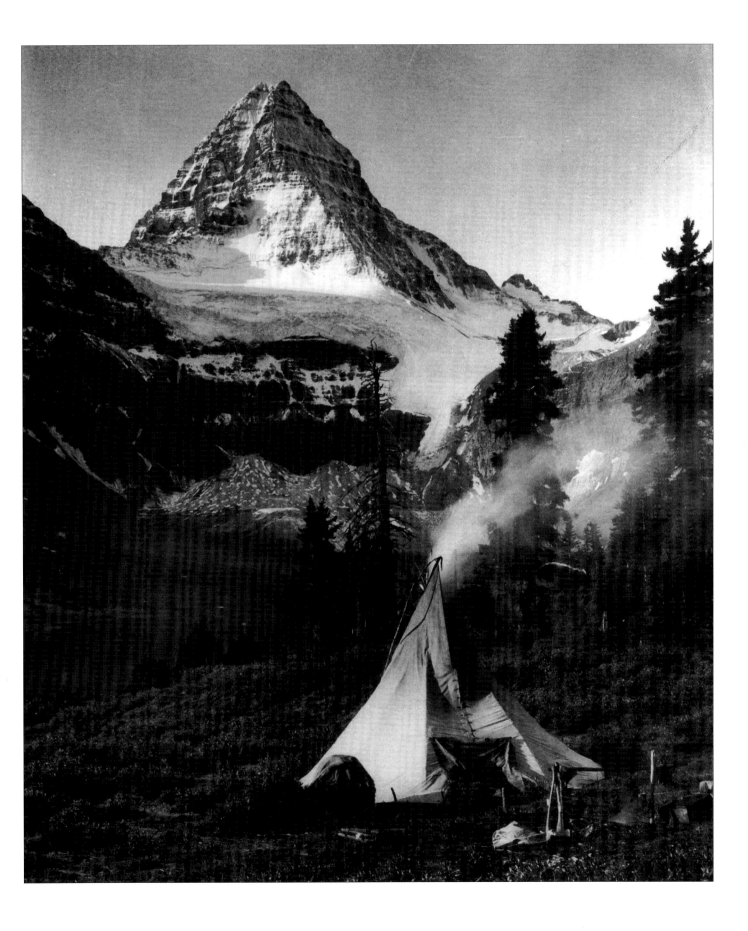

Top:
Castle Mountain
A car heads eastward along the Banff-Winderemere Highway (now known as the Kootenay Parkway) towards Castle Mountain. After World War II this mountain was re-named Mt. Eisenhower in tribute to the famous American General. Its name reverted to Castle Mountain in the 1990s due to its historic significance.

Bottom:
Chateau Lake Louise
An early edition of the Chateau Lake Louise adopted a Tudor style of architecture. This version could house 500 guests and featured electric lighting, steam heat and elaborate dining facilities. It was destroyed by a massive fire on July 3, 1924.
photo ca. 1909

Opposite:
A Native Chief poses on the shore of Lake Louise in this promotion photograph taken for the Canadian Pacific Railway. Mt. Victoria and the Victoria Glacier provide the lofty backdrop.

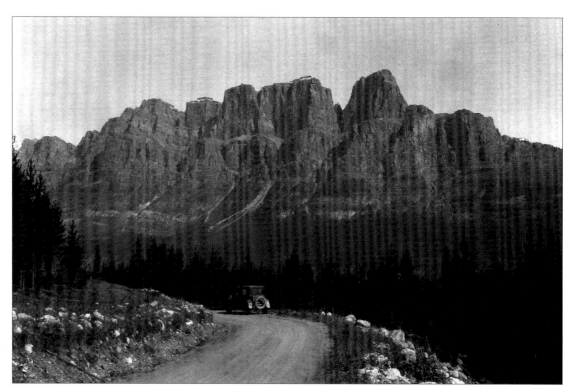

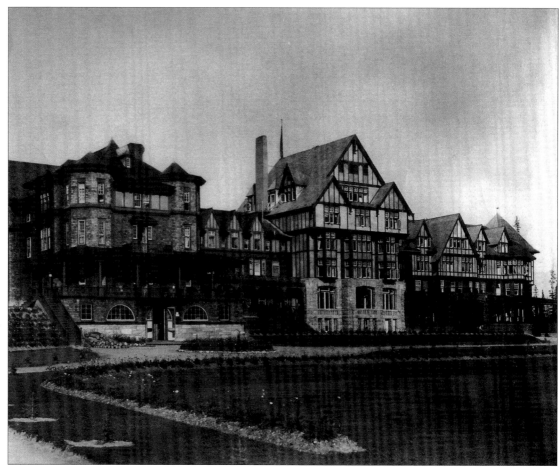

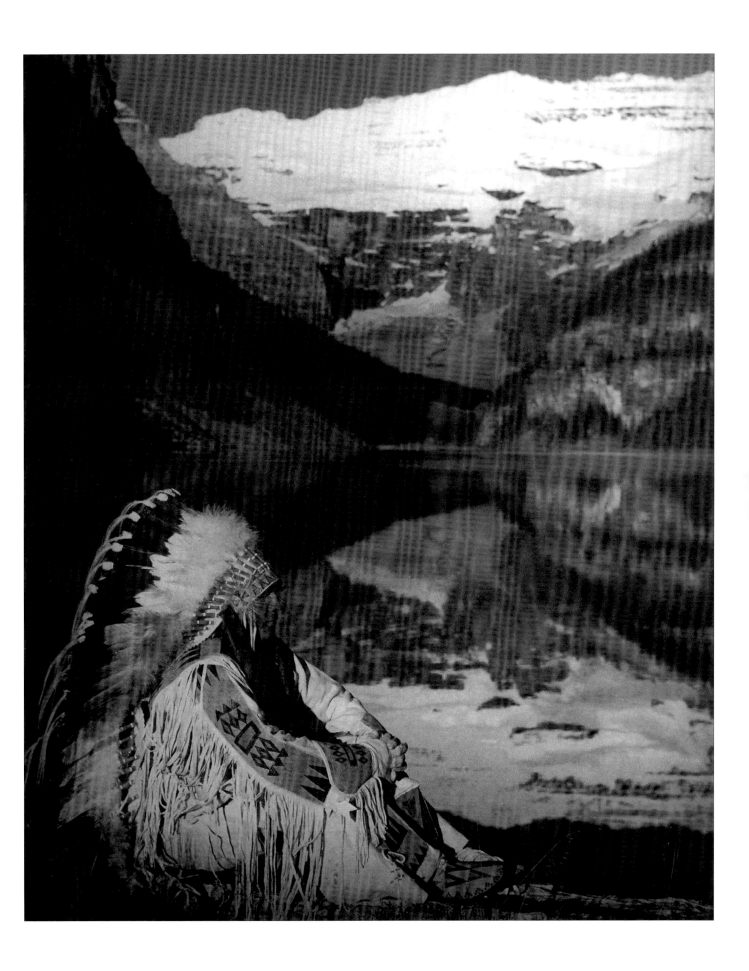

Top:
Maligne Lake
A teepee nestles on the shore of Maligne Lake in Jasper National Park in this Byron Harmon photo. Harmon frequently used a teepee for added dramatic and pictorial effect.
photo ca. 1924

Bottom:
The Lounge in Jasper Park Lodge
This magnificent lounge, complete with stuffed animal heads, wicker furniture and an open log structure, graced the interior of the Jasper Park Lodge, a Canadian National Railway hotel.
photo ca. 1925

Opposite:
Mt. Assiniboine
At 3618m/11,870 ft, Mt. Assiniboine is one of the highest peaks in the Rockies, and Mt. Assiniboine Provincial Park is one of the most popular hiking destinations. The scenery in the Assiniboine Valley is spectacular.

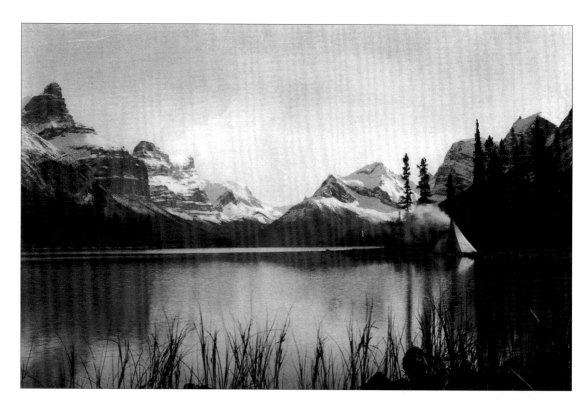

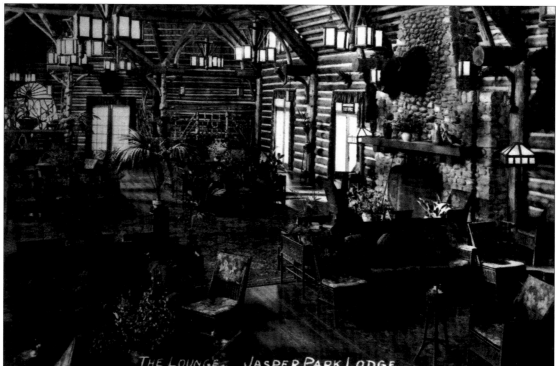

THE LOUNGE. JASPER PARK LODGE.

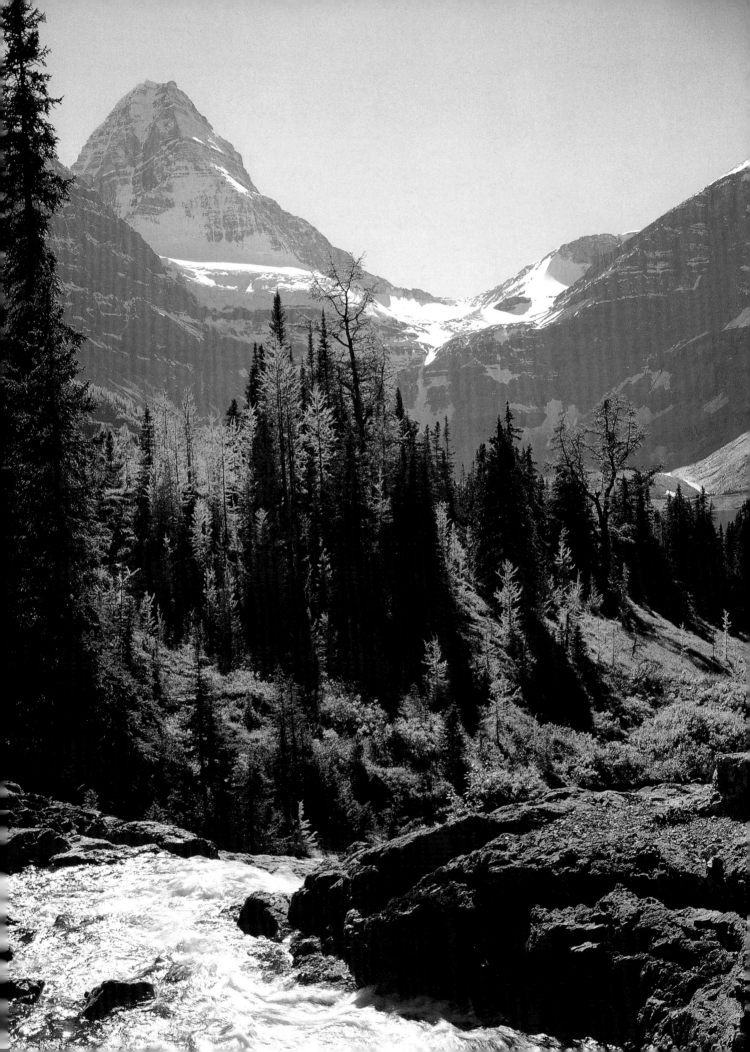

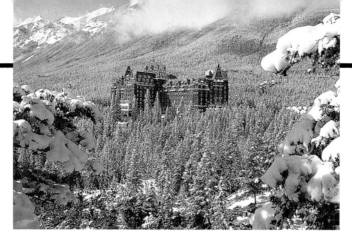

The Canadian Rockies

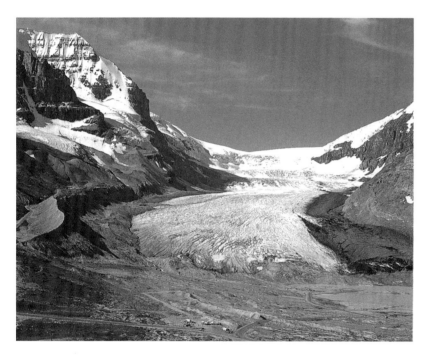

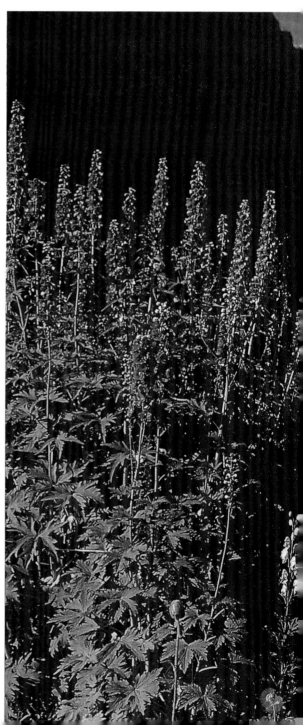

Top:
The Fairmont Banff Springs Hotel
No matter what the season, this world-famous "Castle in the Mountains" in the town of Banff is both welcoming and exciting.

Above:
Athabasca Glacier
Located along the Icefield Parkway, this active glacier flows from the Columbia Icefield. It is one of the most popular landmarks in the Rockies. Snowmobile tours allow visitors an up-close experience of this amazing wonder.

Introduction

The Canadian Rockies are known world-wide for their incredible alpine beauty including stunning bleach-white glaciers, pristine turquoise lakes, raging mountain rivers, and towering waterfalls. The Rockies are home to two major resort towns — Banff and Jasper — as well as two active and thriving villages — Lake Louise and Field.

Put this all together and you have one of the special places on the planet, a place where tourist and wilderness adventurer co-exist, a place where aesthetics and survival go hand-in-hand.

The book begins with historical photographs of bygone eras that set the stage for the more contemporary portrait of the Rockies. The colour pages proceed from south to north, starting from Waterton Lakes National Park and finishing with Jasper National Park and Mt. Robson.

One of the exciting features of this particualr alpine world is the wild animals that one meets along the way. Therefore, included are pictures of some of the magnificent wildlife frequently encountered along the trails or next to the roads and parkways.

Below
Lake Louise and Victoria Glacier
This lake is one of the iconic landmarks of the Canadian Rockies. It is known through-out the world for its magnificent compositional symmetry, its startlingly clear colours and its thundering avalanches.

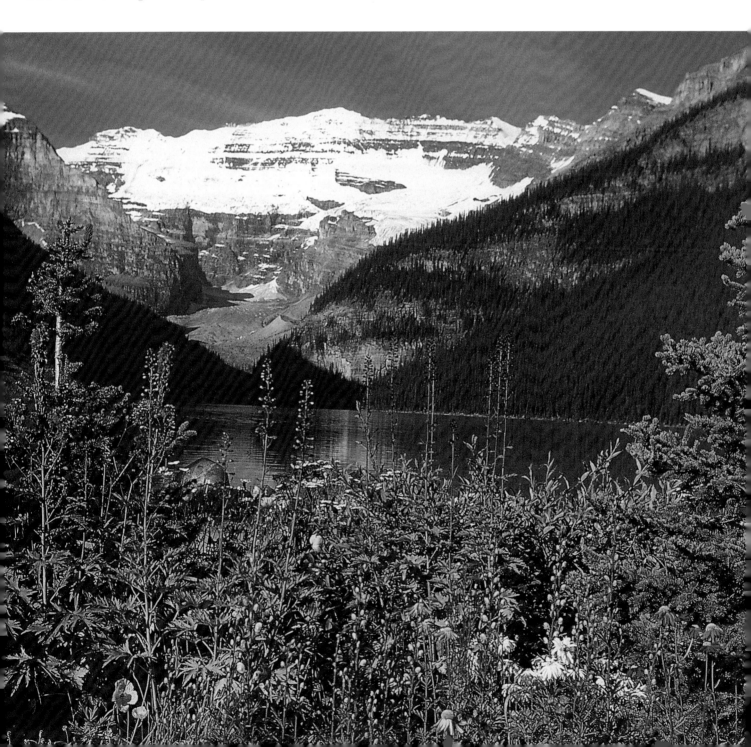

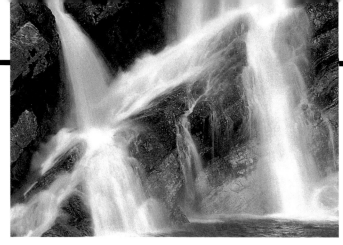

Waterton

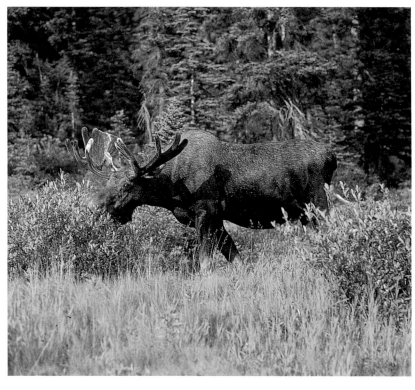

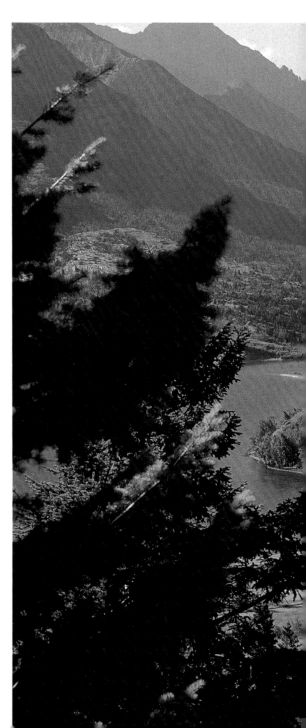

Top:
Cameron Falls
A walk around Waterton townsite is an ideal introduction to Waterton Lakes National Park, and Cameron Falls makes a good starting point. Follow Cameron Falls Drive to the parking lot at the bridge over Cameron Creek.

Above:
Moose in a sunny field
Although normally reclusive, these huge animals can sometimes be spotted feeding in the lakes or marshes that dot the Canadian Rockies.

Waterton became a national park in 1911. In 1932, Waterton and its neighbour – Glacier National Park in Montana, USA – were dedicated as an International Peace Park. Because of the way mountain building happened in this area, Waterton is literally a place where peaks meet prairie. The effect is stunning. In addition to gorgeous views, you'll find great hiking, fishing and boating. A full range of services is available at the townsite during the summer months. Waterton is known for its windy climate and the incredible variety of its plant and animal life. More than one half of the plant species in Alberta can be found here.

The average elevations of mountain summits in Waterton are lower than in the other parks, and the peaks are more irregular in shape. Some of the rocks are among the oldest visible in the Rockies – an incredible one and a half billion years old. There are no glaciers here now, but the mountains and valleys owe much of their appearance to the effects of glaciation. Upper Waterton Lake, for instance, occupies a glacially scoured trough. With a depth of 150 m/492 ft, this is the deepest lake in the Rockies.

Popular short hikes in Waterton include Blakiston Falls, Bison Viewpoint, Red Rock Canyon, Crandell Lake, Bear's Hump and Prince of Wales. Many lakes are popular for sport fishing, with various species of trout comprising most of the catch. Motorized boats may be launched on the Upper and Middle Waterton Lakes, and boat tours are offered on Upper Waterton.

Below:
The Prince of Wales Hotel
With its gorgeous view of Waterton Lake, the deepest lake in the Canadian Rockies and one of the most beautiful, the Prince of Wales Hotel has a lot to offer its guests. It was built in 1926.

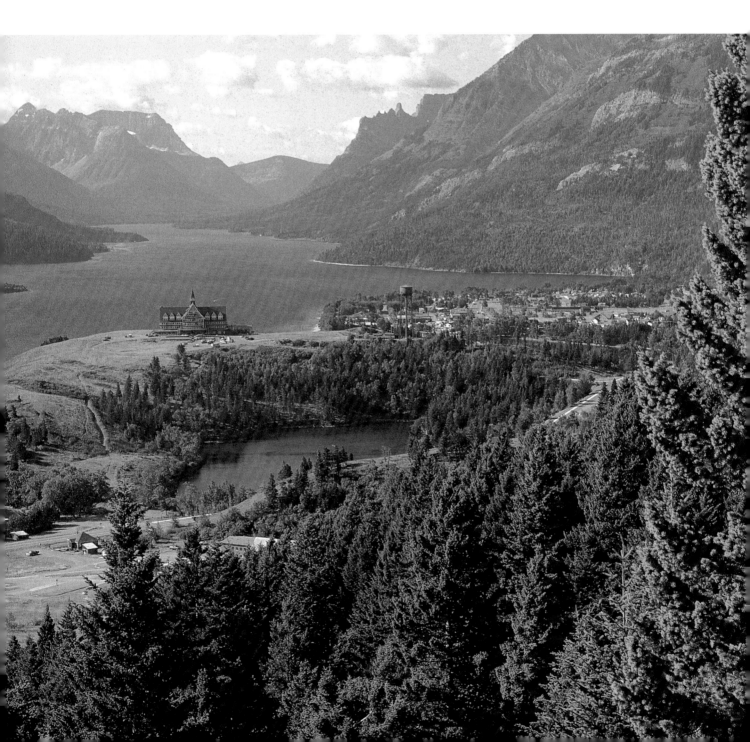

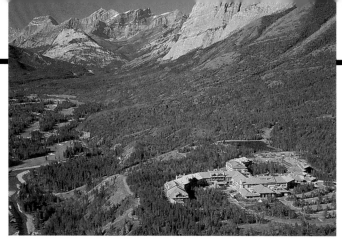

Kananaskis

Top:

Kananaskis Village and Mt. Kidd

This year-round resort features three hotels, two golf courses, tennis and skiing. Mt. Allan, site of the alpine skiing events during the 1988 Winter Olympics, is right next door.

Right:

The Three Sisters

Canmore's most famous landmark can be seen from the town and the highway. Canmore was the site of the Nordic skiing events during the 1988 Winter Olympic Games, and the Nordic Centre is now open year-round for public use.

Opposite:

The Kananaskis Golf Course

Kananaskis Country is Albertans' backyard mountain park, and it's very well-equipped. Visitors can choose from a wide range of recreational opportunities, including a 36-hole world-class golf course.

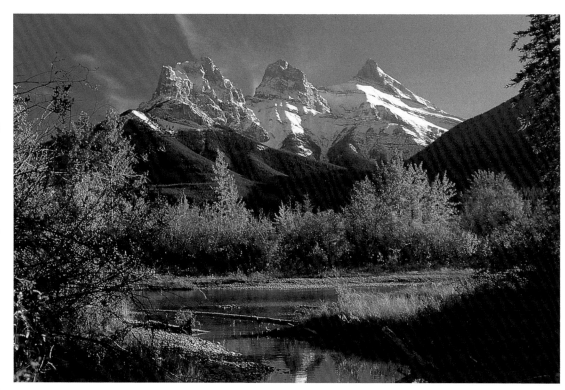

Kananaskis Country is a vast 4250 sq km/1640 sq mi recreational area encompassing mountains, forests, grasslands, lakes and rivers on the eastern slopes of the Canadian Rockies, including Kananaskis Provincial Park. Developed and operated since 1978 by the Alberta government, it was created 'to alleviate congestion in National Parks and to provide greater recreation opportunities for Albertans.' And it does both, although so far the area is visited less often than the national parks.

K-Country is a year-round resort area. Hiking trails abound, as do campgrounds, bicycle paths, and lakes and streams for those who like to fish and boat. The 36-hole

Kananaskis Country golf course is one of the most spectacular in western Canada. Deer and elk, especially, like its velvety fairways.

If you like high country, try the summit of Highwood Pass, reputedly the highest pass crossed by a road in Canada. At this ear-popping height, your eyes are level with the tree line.

In 1988, thousands upon thousands of spectators converged on the Mt. Allan area to watch athletes from around the world compete in the downhill events of the XVth Winter Olympic Games. The Nordic events took place up the road at Canmore.

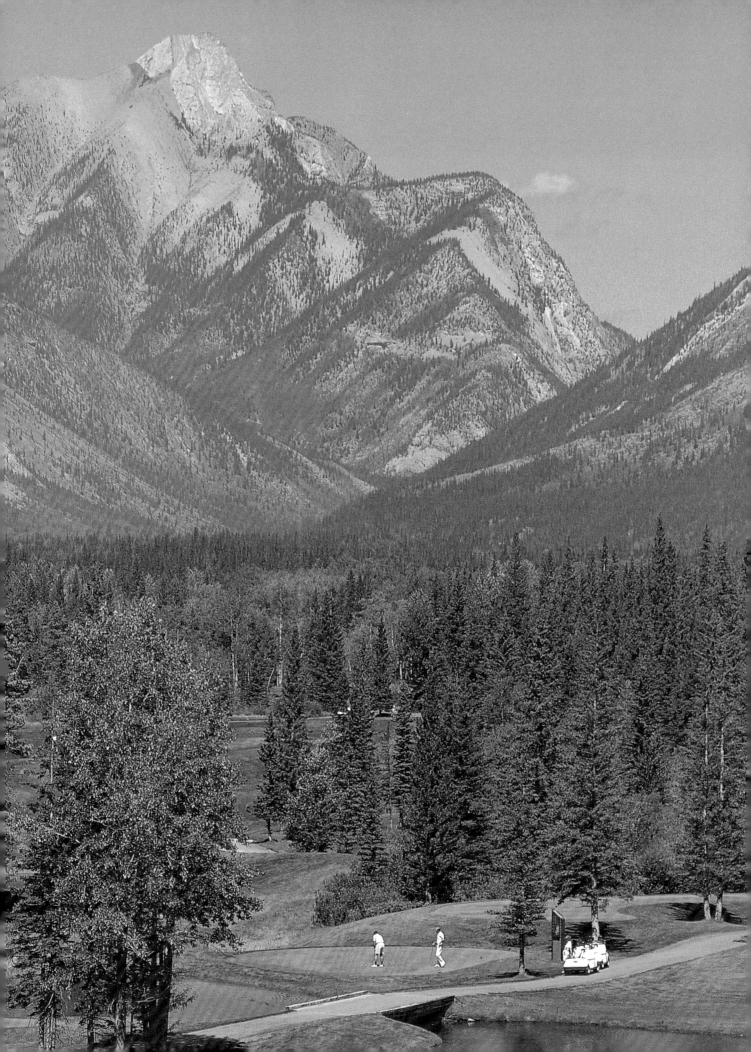

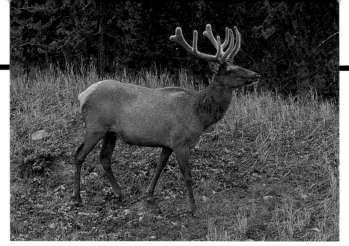

Banff

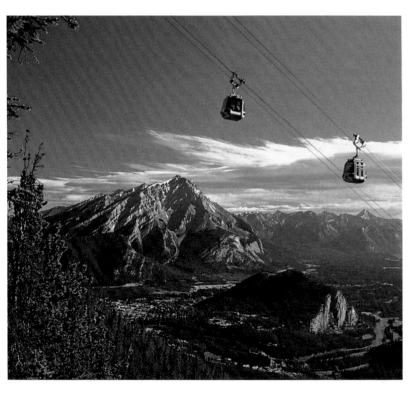

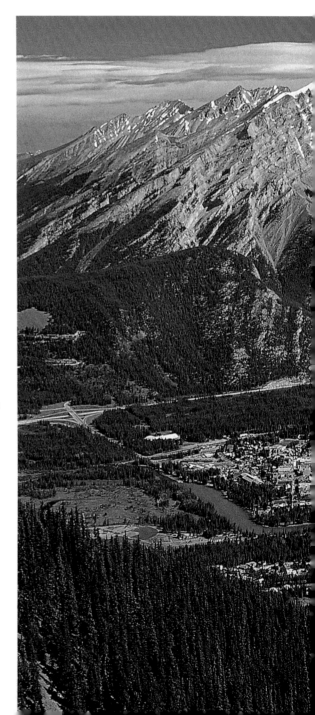

Top:
Wandering Wapiti
The Native name for elk is wapiti, which means 'white rump.' The Bow Valley is ideal habitat for elk, and most visitors will have an opportunity to see one wandering along, perhaps even in the town of Banff itself.

Above:
The Banff Gondola
Ride to the top of Sulphur Mountain for a fabulous view of the town of Banff. The Banff Gondola provides a dramatic and comfortable way to experience a view normally available only for mountaineers.

Banff is known around the world, from Asia to Europe and across Canada, as a place where some of the most beautiful, mountainous land on the planet can be found. Banff National Park is visited by over three million people every year, and it seems unlikely that very many of them go home disappointed. It's true that the crowds can be a bit thick in the height of summer, but there's so much to make up for that here that most people take the odd traffic jam in stride.

The 6641 sq km/2564 sq mi of land protected in Banff National Park is a wilderness of soaring mountains, glaciers, and blue-green lakes and rivers. Evergreen forests are interspersed with larch trees that turn gold in the fall, and dozens of varieties of wildflowers bloom in alpine meadows. Hundreds of animals and birds live here, and it's not at all uncommon to see elk or deer grazing at the side of the road, even very close to Banff.

Mineral hot springs also occur naturally in the park. Although they're now just one of the reasons people come here, they hold a very important place in the park's history. Before the era of plumbing, a hot bath was a hard thing to come by in the wild west; and the discovery in 1883 of naturally occurring hot springs looked like a money-maker to the three Canadian Pacific Railway workers who stumbled on what is now known as the Cave and Basin Hot Springs. However, the CPR workers' dreams of fame and fortune quickly went up in the smoke of an ugly dispute that arose over ownership of the springs. To settle the matter, in 1885 the federal government stepped in to

Below:
The Town of Banff from Sulphur Mountain
Banff is nestled in the beautiful Bow River Valley. Cascade Mountain provides the spectacular backdrop. This is the view from the top of the Sulphur Mountain gondola ride.

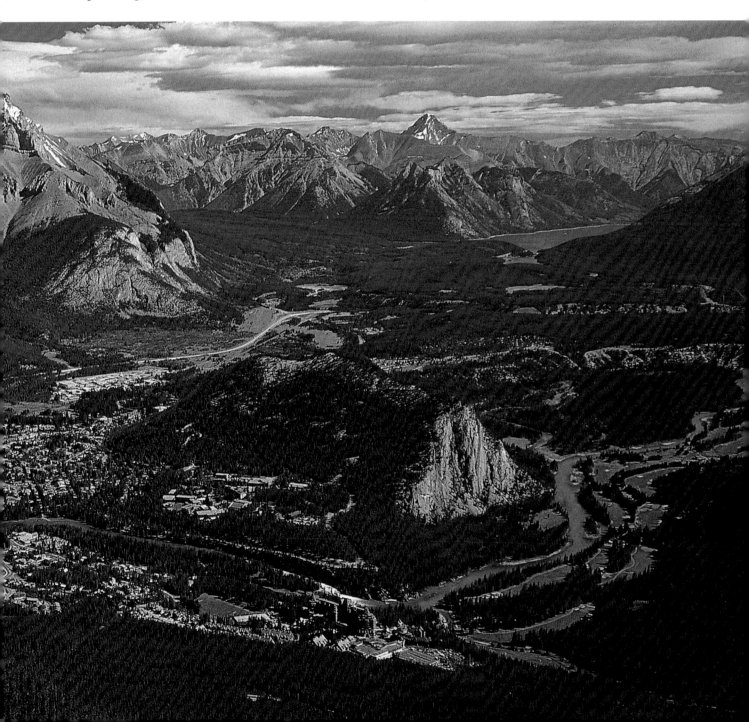

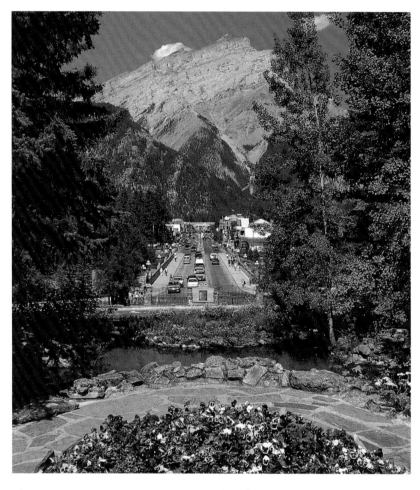

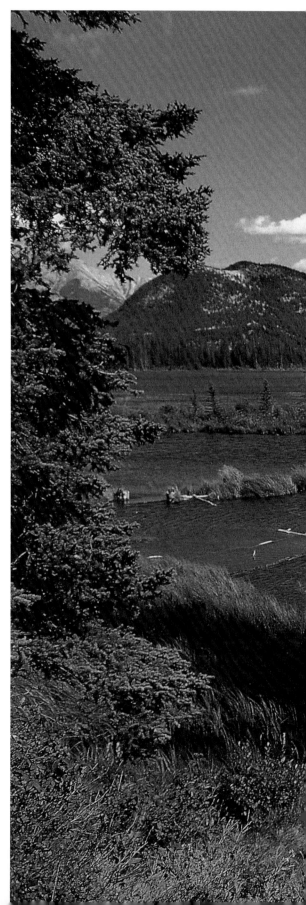

Above:
Cascade Mountain from the Cascade Gardens
The mountain that Banff Avenue seems to lead to was named by James Hector in 1858 as a translation from the Stoney name, which meant 'mountain where the water falls.' When Cascade's waterfalls freeze in winter, they are popular with ice climbers.

Opposite:
Mt. Rundle and Vermilion Lake
This is another classic Canadian Rockies view. The shallow Vermilion Lakes are excellent habitat for beaver and for many birds. If you want to have a closer look at the lake, follow Vermilion Lakes Drive and take a walk on the self-guiding Fenland Trail.

create Canada's first national park. It was 26 sq km in size.

Over time the boundaries of the park were expanded, and a railway connecting one end of Canada to the other was constructed. Once the track was laid, the CPR lost little time in building the Banff Springs Hotel in 1888 and then, at the turn of the century, Chateau Lake Louise. Wealthy and distinguished visitors swarmed to the new luxury resorts deep in the Canadian wilderness. When the first road between Banff and Lake Louise was opened in 1920, the entire valley was thrown open to an additional flood of visitors from across Canada, the United States and beyond.

Today, new attractions and new facilities are constantly being added for the year-round enjoyment and convenience of those who come to one of the world's most popular tourist destinations. While Banff owes its popularity among world travellers primarily to the mag-

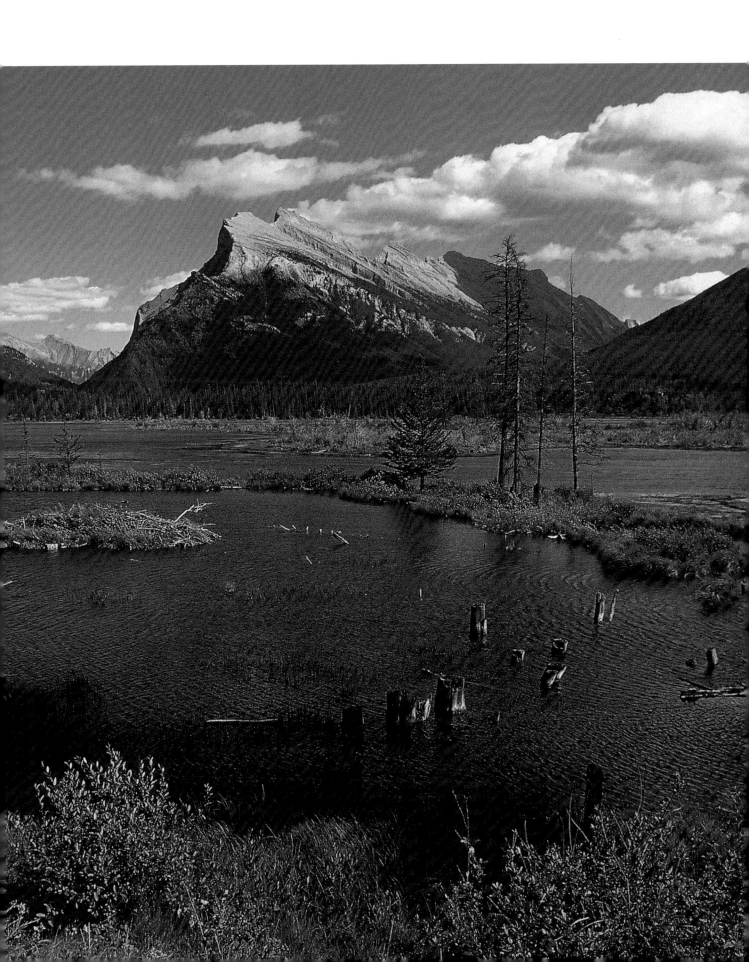

nificent wilderness which surrounds it, there is no shortage of things to do and see in the thriving town itself. All you need to take in most of it is a good pair of walking shoes.

Internationally renowned, The Banff Centre, a few short blocks from the downtown core, offers a wide variety of fine arts courses and events ranging from recitals to major dramatic and musical productions. The summer season is highlighted by the Banff Festival of the Arts, which runs from May to August.

Don't miss the handsome Whyte Museum of the Canadian Rockies, home of Banff's colourful archives and host to exhibitions by outstanding artists. You'll find it on Bear Street. A short distance away, across the Bow River, the Luxton Museum on Cave Avenue tells the story of the Plains Indians who roamed the area long before the first train whistle ever echoed among the nearby mountains.

Also worth a visit is the Cave and Basin Centennial Centre, which houses the newly renovated bathing pools as well as the original bath house built in 1887. This is the historical heart of Banff, known through the years to royalty, millionaires and movie stars. The Upper Hot Springs are also popular for a good

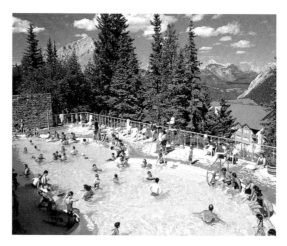

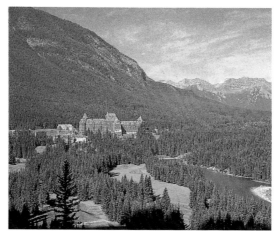

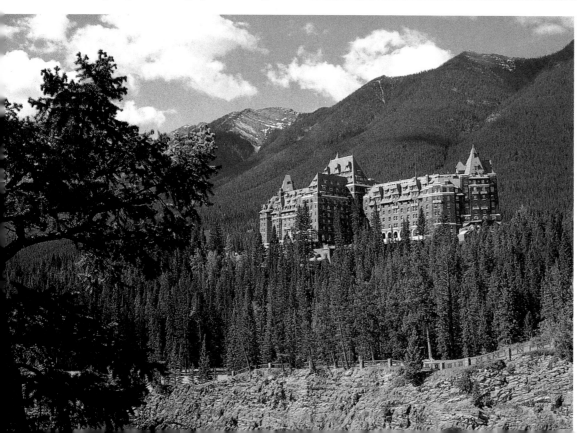

Top:

The Sulphur Mountain Hot Springs
After a day of hiking or skiing, there's nothing quite like a soak in a mineral hot springs pool. The Upper Hot Springs pool, shown here, is one of two developed hot springs in Banff. The waters here are hotter than at the Cave and Basin.

Middle:

The Fairmont Banff Springs Hotel and the Banff Springs Golf Course
The Banff Springs Hotel has one of the most spectacular settings in the world. Surrounded by mountains and evergreen trees, this hotel overlooks the Bow River and its own world-class golf course.

Bottom:

The Fairmont Banff Springs Hotel
When this world-famous hotel was opened in 1888, it was the largest hotel in the world and room rates started at $3.50 per day. Today the Springs can accommodate 1700 guests in its 867 rooms (and room rate have gone up).

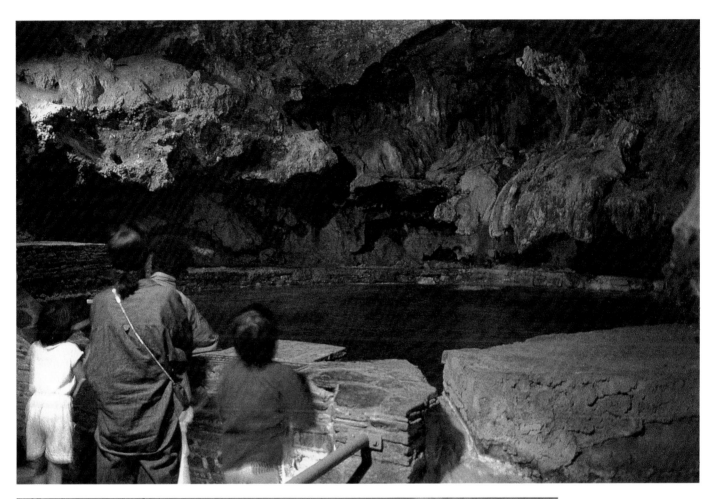

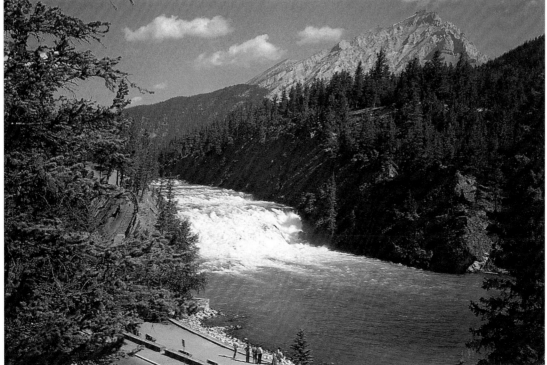

Top:
The Cave and Basin
Over one million people visit this site annually. The Cave and Basin has been one of Banff's premier attractions since the park was founded, and in 1985 the building was reconstructed as part of the National Parks Centennial.

Bottom:
Bow Falls and Cascade Mountain
A visit to Bow Falls is a popular walk from the Fairmont Banff Springs or downtown Banff. The Bow River takes its name from a Native Cree word for bow, in reference to the fact that wood suitable for making hunting bows was found along its banks.

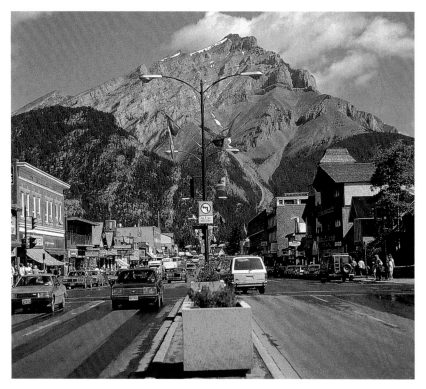

Above:
Banff Avenue
This is the main drag of the biggest town in the mountain parks, and you should be able to find just about anything you might need in the way of supplies here. It's also great for rainy days, thanks to all the museums and gift shops in town.

Opposite:
Mt. Rundle and the Town of Banff
One of the most dramatic views of Mt. Rundle and the Bow Valley is seen from the viewpoint on the road to the Mt. Norquay ski area. Rundle's cliffs are nearly a mile/1.6 km high in places, which makes them popular with climbers.

soak after a day of hiking or skiing.

Even today, international celebrities can frequently be seen at the 578-room castle that rises from the trees in the shadow of Mt. Rundle, overlooking the townsite. In the spring of 1988, the Banff Springs Hotel celebrated her 100th birthday. Facilities today include a bank, post office, and beauty salon, shops, sauna, tennis courts, and one of the world's most scenic 18-hole golf courses. During the winter, the hotel is a favourite with skiers.

When the time comes to move on to Lake Louise, motorists have a happy choice between two routes. The Trans-Canada Highway (Hwy. 1), following the south shore of the Bow River for all but 6 km/3.7 mi on the outskirts of Banff, is straighter, flatter and faster. The Bow Valley Parkway (Hwy. 1A), across the river, winds uphill and downhill through thick evergreen forests, passing close to several points of particular scenic or historic interest. Consider taking one route on your way to Lake Louise, the other coming back.

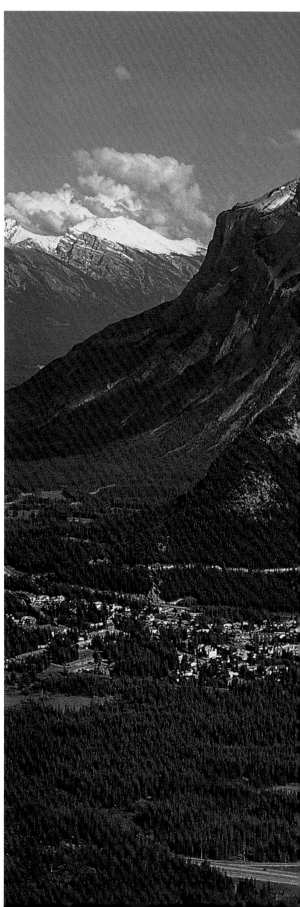

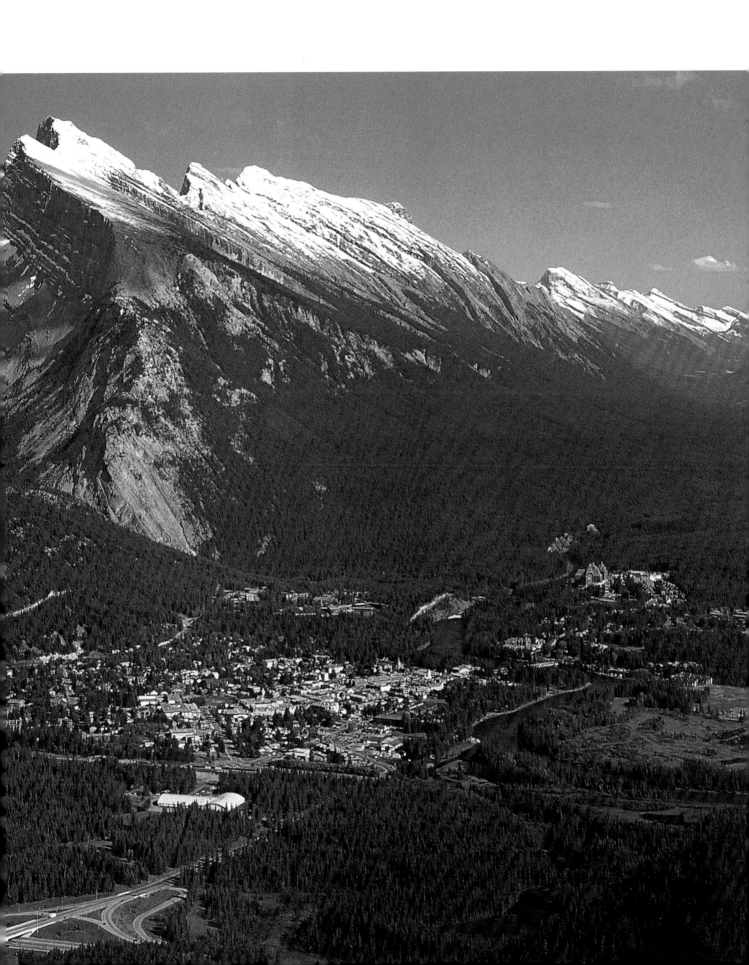

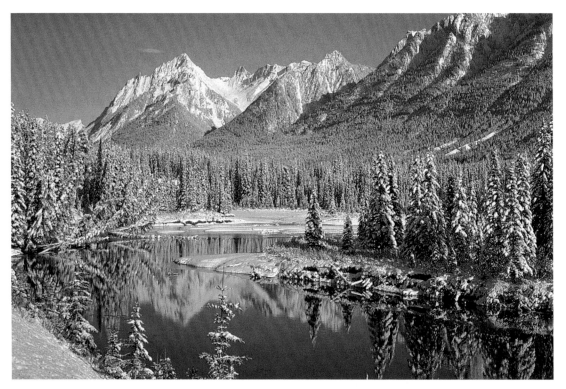

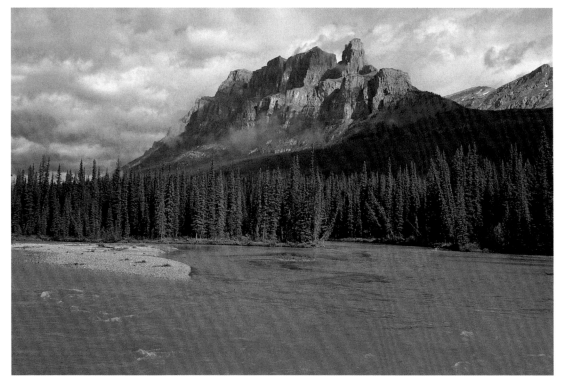

Top left:
The Bow River and the Sawback Range in Winter
The jagged ridges of the Sawback Range parallel the east side of the Bow Valley Parkway between Banff and Castle Junction. The parkway is a slower route to Lake Louise, but it's a really beautiful drive.

Bottom left:
Castle Mountain and the Bow River
It's easy to see how Castle Mountain got its name. You pass it on the way to Lake Louise via the Trans-Canada Highway, which is the faster route. Like Mt. Rundle's, Castle's cliffs are popular with climbers.

Opposite:
The Lower Falls of Johnston Canyon
Johnston Canyon is 30 m/98 ft deep in places, and an ingenious walkway allows visitors to travel into its depths. The lower falls are only half as high as the upper falls, which are 1.6 km further up the trail.

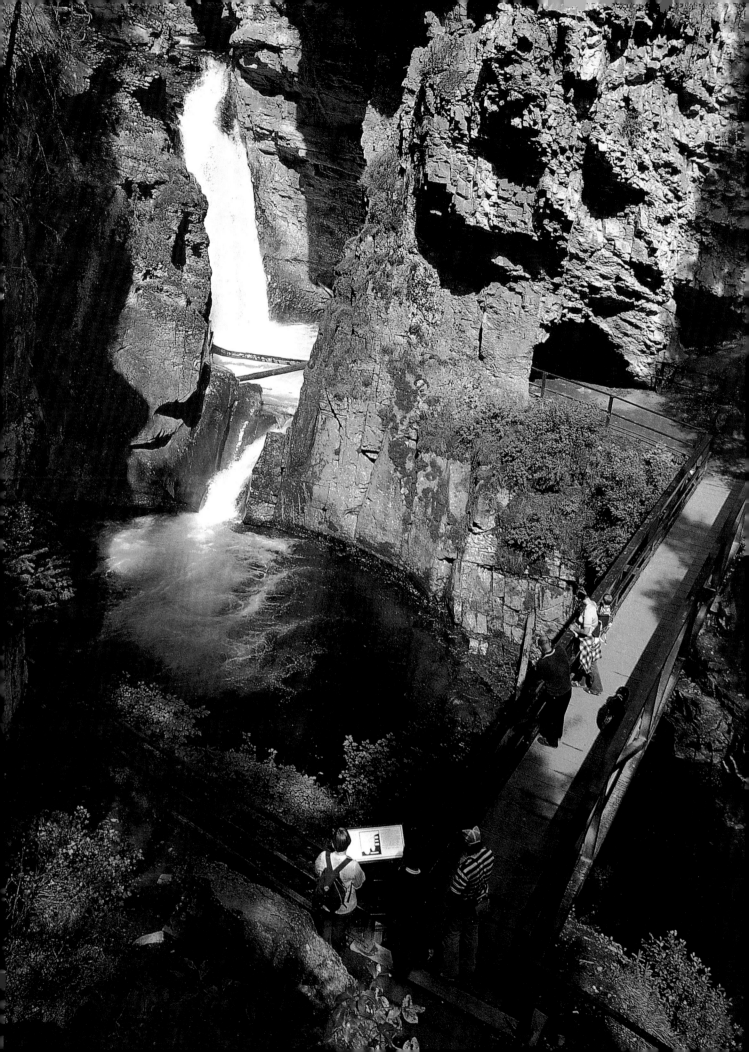

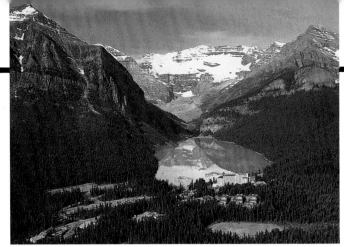

Lake Louise

Young Tom Wilson was working with a railway survey crew during the summer of 1883. One night he heard the rumbling roar of an avalanche, uncomfortably close to his campsite on the Pipestone River. From a Stoney guide, he learned that the source of the thunder was a great snow mountain that towered above the 'Lake of Little Fishes.' At first light, the two men set out to take a look.

What Wilson found was a spectacle so majestic and moving that he thought he could improve on the Native name, and he christened his discovery 'Emerald Lake' for its startling colour.

But that name didn't last either. When the Geographical Board of Canada heard about this wondrous mountain jewel, they decided to call it Lake Louise after Princess Louise Caroline Alberta, daughter of Queen Victoria and wife of Canada's Governor-General, the Marquis of Lorne.

Its fame spread rapidly. In 1890 the CPR built a modest chalet on the lakeshore facing Mt. Victoria. By the end of the century the chalet had been expanded to a two-storey frame building, which became the centre for climbing expeditions by adventurers from near and far. In 1924 the first Chateau Lake Louise was almost totally destroyed by fire. and was replaced by the present structure.

Commencing in 1986, a complete redevelopment of the Chateau was undertaken. Today, with the addition of the Glacier Wing, up to 1000 guests can be accommodated year-round. Gone is the tramway that in early days transported visitors between the train station and the hotel – it was dismantled in 1930 in favour of a road. But a new entrance lobby, indoor parking lot and retail area have been added, and the hotel and its grounds are worth a look even if you aren't staying there.

As with many large lakes in the Rockies, the water in Lake Louise comes from glaciers. In the height of summer the temperature of the water might reach 4°C/7.2°F. Its remarkable colour is caused by fine particles of suspended till called rock flour, which reflect the blue/green spectrum of light. People sometimes suspect that photos of Lake Louise have been retouched, until they see the lake for themselves.

Canoes are available for tours of the lake, and horses can be hired for outings along any number of mountain trails near the Chateau. In the spring, blooms of all shapes and colours sprout from garden beds by the lake's shore and along well-groomed walkways. The gondola lift operated by the Lake Louise ski area provides a wonderful panoramic view of Lake Louise, the Chateau and the surrounding mountains.

By early fall the first snows come to Lake Louise, and with them the first skiers to test the slopes and trails in the vast ski area across the lake from Bow Valley. Many head for Skoki Lodge, a small log building built on the valley's eastern rim by cross-country enthusiasts in the early 1930's. Lake Louise is one of Canada's largest ski areas, covering 28 sq km/11 sq mi with over 40 marked runs. This area gets about 418 cm/165 in of snow each winter, so if the snow has been good and the weather holds the ski season can extend into April.

Over the years, some 68 km/42 mi of hiking trails have been carved through the timber and over the rock surrounding Lake Louise. One of the most popular is a 5.5 km/3.4 mi hike to the

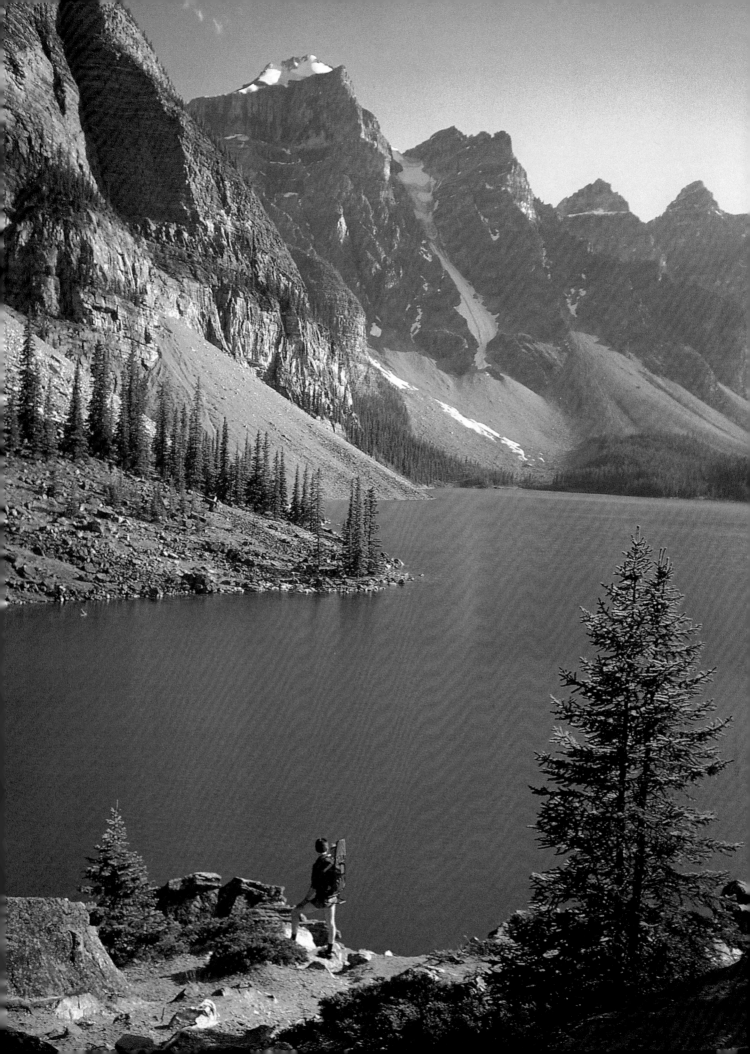

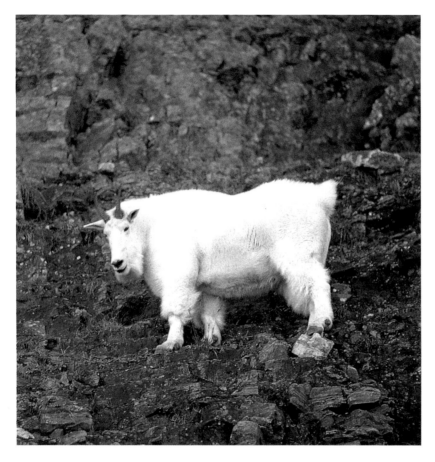

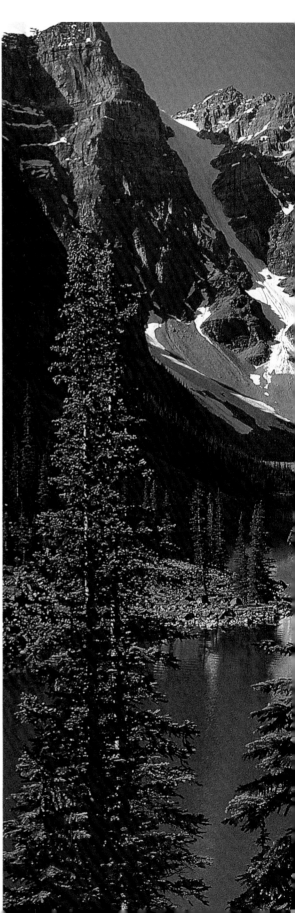

Above:
Mountain Goat Smiling
Although it seems like a difficult place to hang out, this mountain goat is perfectly at home on the cliff's edge. Baby mountain goats are able to walk on the day they are born, and follow their mothers over the most dizzying of terrain.

Opposite:
Moraine Lake
This is one of the most outstanding views in all of the Canadian Rockies. You can see this view if you stand on the shore of the "Rock Pile" at the end of Moraine Lake.

Plain of Six Glaciers, where in summertime a tea house offers light lunches, refreshments and a splendid view of Mt. Lefroy, The Mitre and Mt. Victoria. The round trip takes about five hours. Another highly popular jaunt takes you to Lake Agnes, just 3.5 km/2.2 mi away. For many people, though, a stroll around Lake Louise itself is enough of an outing – the gentle shoreline trail is just under 2 km/1.2 mi long, and it's wheelchair accessible.

Moraine Lake and the Wenkchemna Peaks lie to the south of Lake Louise, about 12 km/ 7.5 mi down the road. Some claim that Moraine Lake was misnamed by Walter Wilcox, the explorer who discovered it. He thought it was hemmed in at one end by a moraine: glacial debris that piles up to form a natural dam over a long period of time. According to the experts, Moraine Lake was really formed by an enormous rock slide that crashed down from the nearby Tower of Babel. But moraine

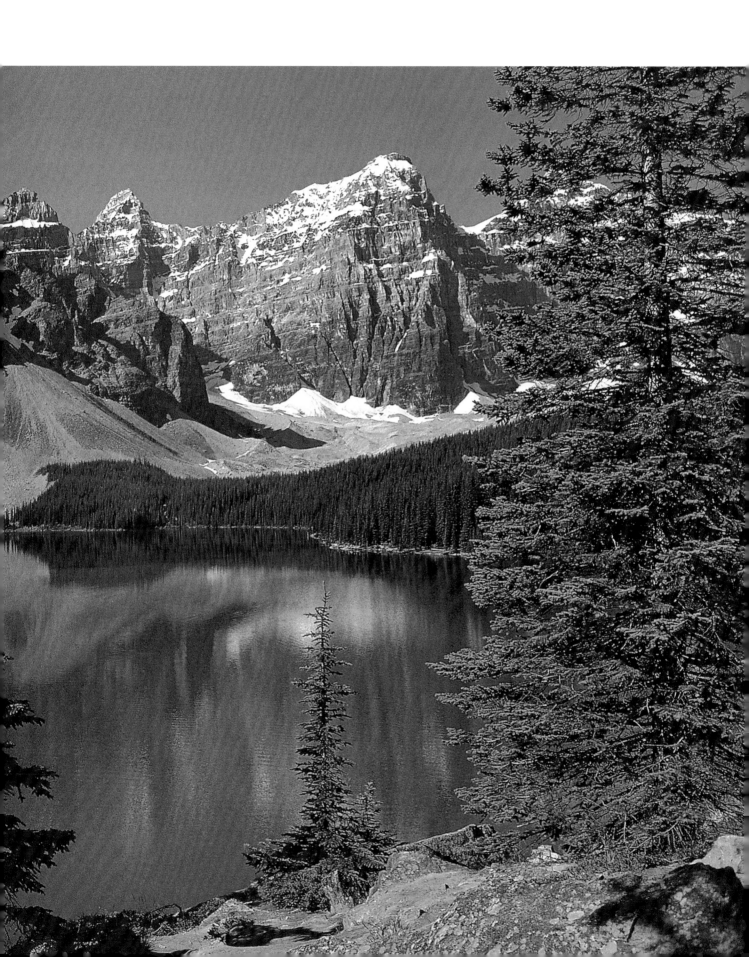

Top Right:
Skiing the Hard Way in the Canadian Rockies
Weather you're into downhill or cross-country, deep powder is a challenge. And the Canadian Rockies get plenty of it, because they get lots of snow - about 418 cm/165 inches each winter in the Lake Louise area.

Middle right:
Fairmont Lake Louise in Winter
Chateau Lake Louise is open year round, and it's very beautiful here when snow blankets the mountains. The lake freezes from November through June.

Bottom right:
The Fairmont Chateau Lake Louise at Night
Redevelopment that began in 1986 has boosted the Chateau's capacity to 1000 guests. The new Glacier Wing was constructed, along with a new entrance lobby, retail area and indoor parking lot.

Opposite:
The Fairmont Chateau Lake Louise Grounds
Like many lakes in the Rockies, Lake Louise's waters are glacial in origin. The remarkable colour of the water is caused by fine particles of suspended till called rock flour, which reflect the blue/green spectrum of light.

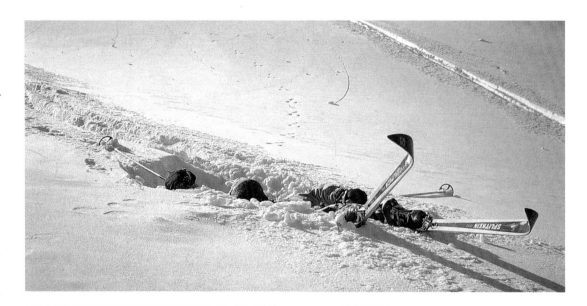

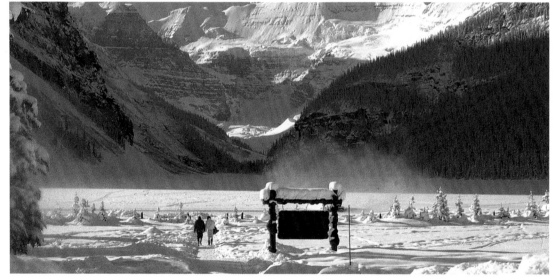

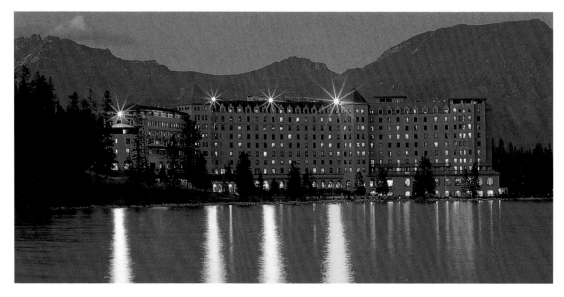

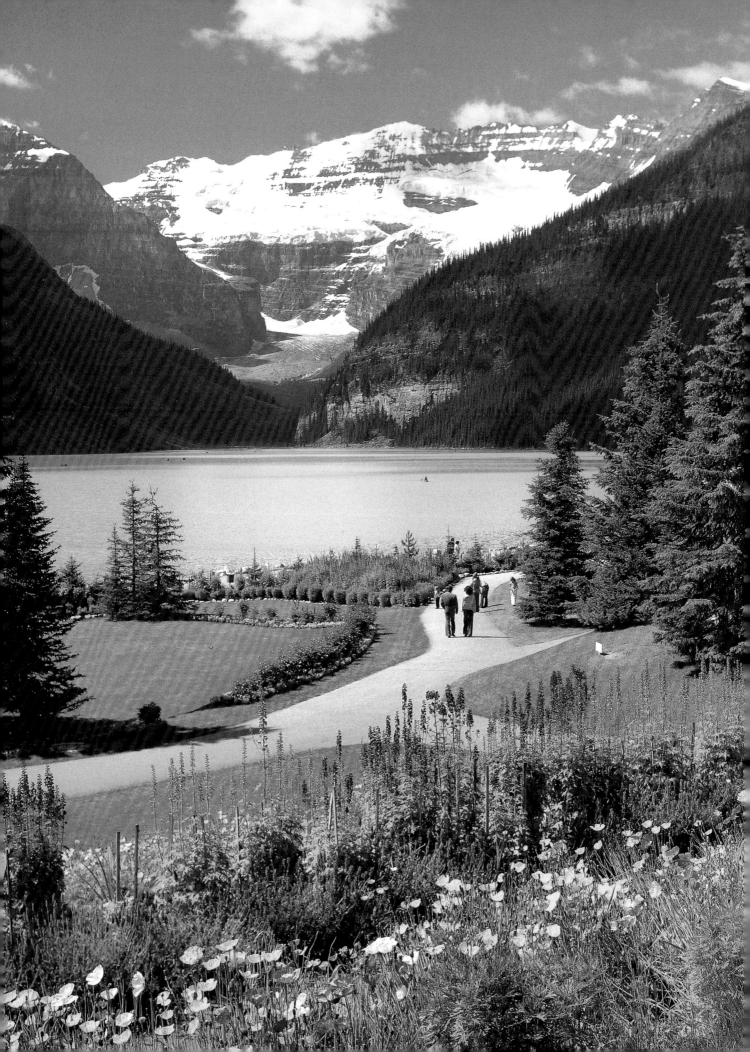

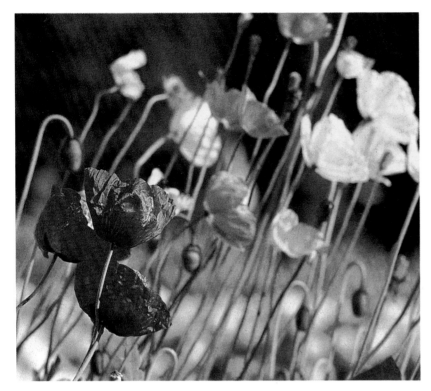

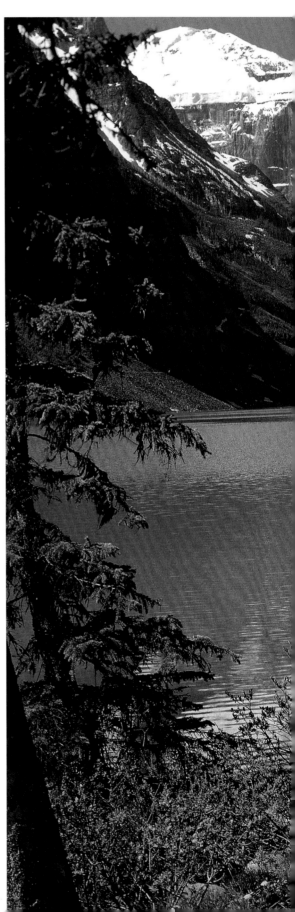

Above:

Poppies at Lake Louise
The Fairmont Chateau Lake Louise's famous gardens include the Icelandic poppy, which is native to Siberia and thus well-suited to the short summers here.

Opposite:

Lake Louise and the Lakeside Trail
Don't miss this peaceful walk along the northwest edge of Lake Louise if you can help it. It's only 1.9 km long and it's wheelchair accessible. This trail branches off to the Plain of Six Glaciers trail also, which is a bit more challenging.

or no moraine, this is one of the loveliest areas in the Rockies for a day of hiking, photography or just drinking in the sights. The Moraine Lake Lodge provides boat rentals, accommodation and an excellent restaurant.

One of the most popular hikes in the Moraine Lake area leads to Larch Valley, which is nestled between Pinnacle Mountain and Mt. Temple. The valley is named for the tree Lyall's larch, an uncommon coniferous tree that grows in scattered mountainous areas of southern Alberta and BC. In early fall, the larch's needles turn yellow and gold, and turn this valley into a photographer's paradise. Strong hikers can climb beyond Larch Valley to the crest of Sentinel Pass, which is, at 2611 m/8564 ft, the highest point reached by trail in the mountain national parks.

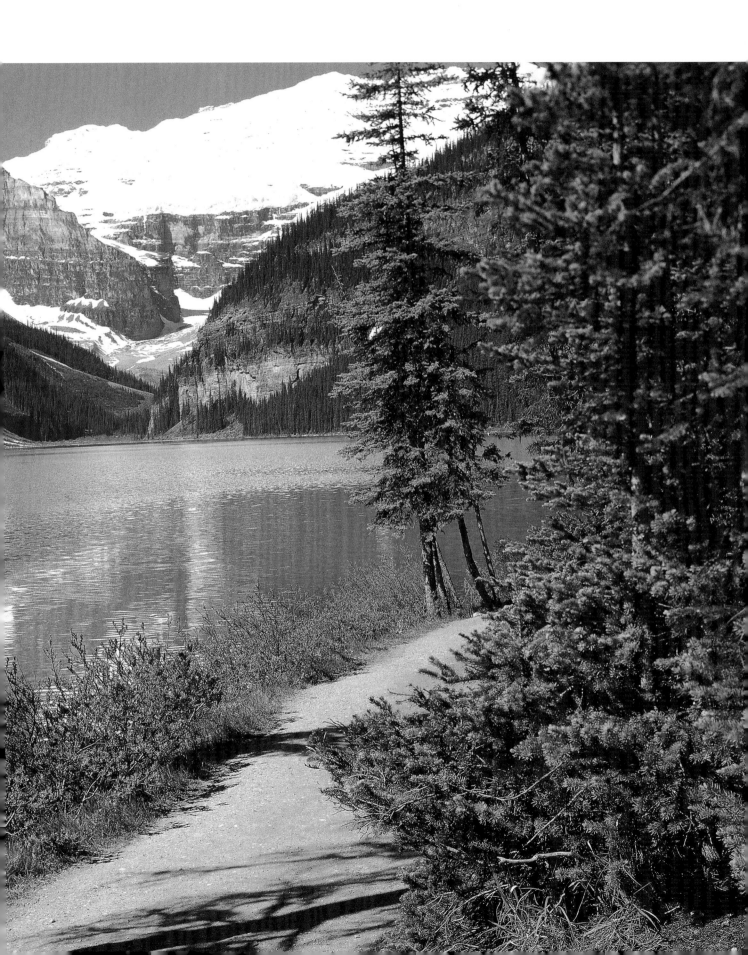

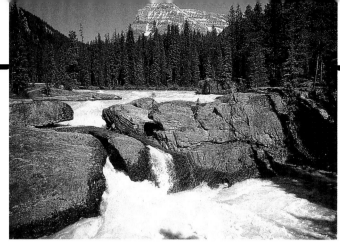

Yoho

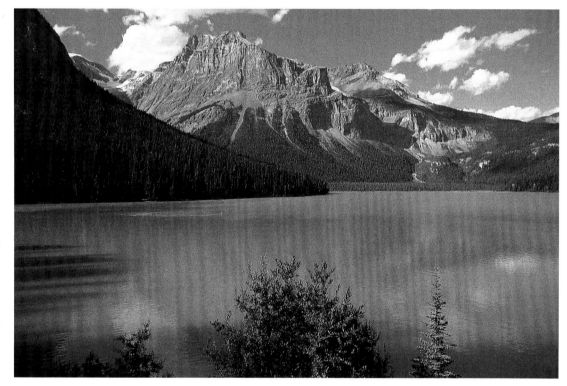

Top:
The Natural Bridge and Mt. Stephen
The Kicking Horse River encounters a resistant formation of limestone here, but it has managed to erode a small channel through to the other side, creating the Natural Bridge. When the river is running high the bridge is submerged.

Right:
Emerald Lake and Mt. Burgess
The waters of Yoho's largest lake are dammed by an old glacial moraine, atop which sits the Emerald Lake Lodge (which has a popular teahouse). This is a great area for walking – trails lead out from the parking lot.

Opposite:
Takakkaw Falls
At 378 m/1247 ft in height, Takakkaw Falls is one of the highest waterfalls in Canada, and it's one of the reasons Yoho's theme is 'rock walls and waterfalls.' An easy trail at the end of the Yoho Valley Road leads to the falls.

The origin of Yoho National Park is intrinsically connected to the Canadian Pacific Railway, which was completed through the area in 1884. Some historians wonder why the CPR chose this route for the first trans-continental track through the mountains, since other less challenging routes were available. It was an engineering accomplishment of heroic magnitude, and one for which scores of workers lost their lives. The story is told in an exhibit atop the Kicking Horse Pass.

Yoho is a Native expression of awe and wonder. In 1898 German explorer Jean Habel published an account of explorations in the Yoho Valley, and in his descriptions the scenery lived up to the name. Pressure mounted

from the railway, the outfitters and the explorers to enlarge the protected area. This was accomplished in 1901, with the founding of Yoho Park Reserve. National Park status followed in 1911, and since 1930 the park's area has been stable at 1313 sq km.

Yoho may be the smallest of the four mountain national parks, but it has more than its share of spectacular scenery and a very well-developed trail system. The Burgess Shale, one of the world's most fascinating fossil beds, is located on the slopes of Mt. Stephen at Field and near Burgess Pass. Some of the fossilized remains of marine animals found here date back 530 million years. The Burgess Shale was designated a World Heritage Site in 1980.

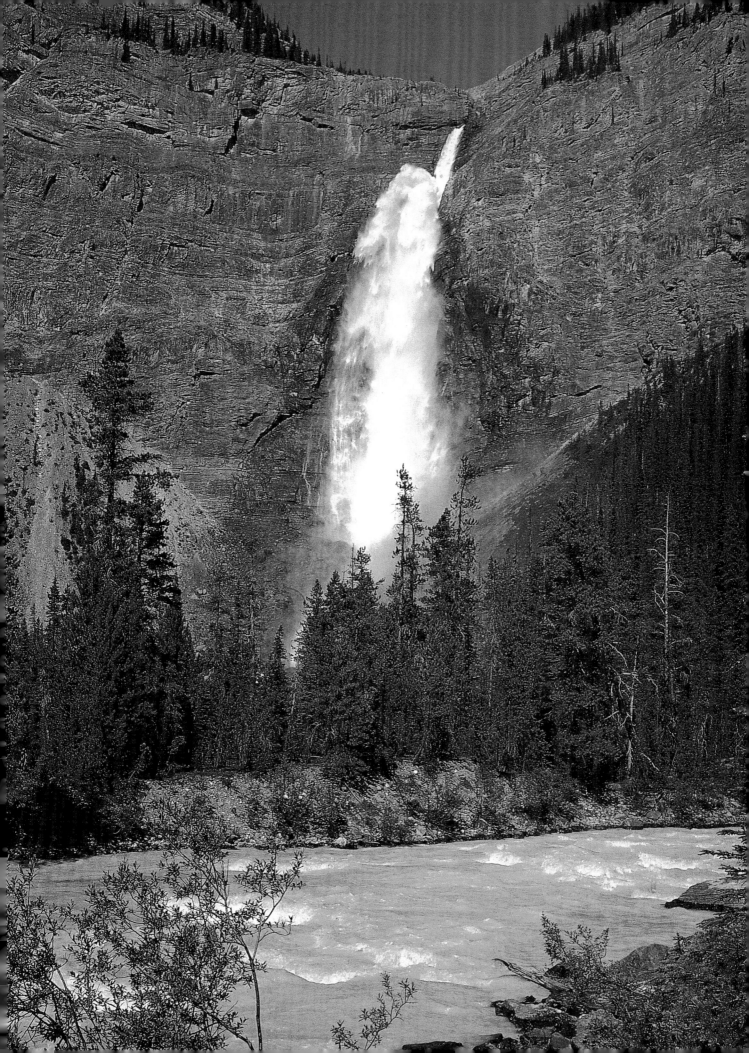

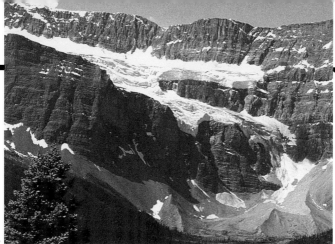

The Icefields

Connoisseurs of extraordinary roads know about the Icefields Parkway, and count it as one of the truly great drives in the world. This is a trip that deserves to be taken slowly, as anyone who has travelled by road from Lake Louise to Jasper will attest.

Construction of the forerunner of the Icefields Parkway began in 1931, as a make-work project during the Great Depression. Crews worked towards each other from Jasper and Lake Louise. When in full swing, the construction involved 625 men. It's incredible to think that very few pieces of machinery were used in overcoming the obstacles presented by the difficult terrain.

The crews met on the hill at the Big Bend in 1939. Their finished product was a 6.5 m/21 ft wide gravel road, 230 km/143 mi in length, which in no place exceeded 8% in grade. The Parkway was first used by autos in 1940, and echoing the words mountaineer Edward Whymper spoke forty years earlier, was heralded in the *Banff Crag and Canyon* as being 'twenty Switzerlands in one.' When the road was upgraded to its present standard in 1961, most of the original grading was retained – a tribute to the quality of the original construction.

The Icefields Parkway travels through the Columbia Icefield, a canopy of interlocking glaciers that spreads over 337 sq km/130 sq mi of land. In places it's close to 365 m/1197 ft thick, and only skilled climbers and guided tours venture out onto its ever-changing surface. At roadside, the average annual snowfall is 6.4 m/21 ft, and on the icefield itself it's over 10 m/32 ft. The road runs very close

to Athabasca Glacier, and it's the one visitors can take a Snowcoach tour on. The history of the glaciers is explained at the Icefield Centre operated by Parks Canada, next to the chalet. A bit farther along you'll find the snowmobile-bus depot.

Parks Canada has done a wonderful job of providing safe and easy access to vantage points from which to observe these icefields, and in explaining their geological and historical significance. There are many roadside exhibits, and well-marked trails lead to canyons, lakes and alpine meadows.

Throughout all but the last mile or so of this section of the Parkway, you are still in Banff National Park. Jasper National Park begins at Sunwapta Pass. If you turn east at Saskatchewan River Crossing on Highway 11, you will come to the eastern boundary about 8 km/5 mi along the road, which then continues on to Rocky Mountain House and the city of Red Deer, Alberta.

The valley of the Howse River, which joins the North Saskatchewan near Saskatchewan River Crossing, was the route that explorer David Thompson used to cross the Great Divide in 1807. Overcoming all manner of obstacles, he pushed on to establish a post for the Northwest Company near what is now the town of Invermere, BC, on the Columbia River. It is ironic that Howse Pass was named for Joseph Howse, a trader with the rival Hudson Bay Company who did not reach the area until three years after Thompson. Now other passes, both to the north and the south, have become the principal arteries used by railway and highway traffic.

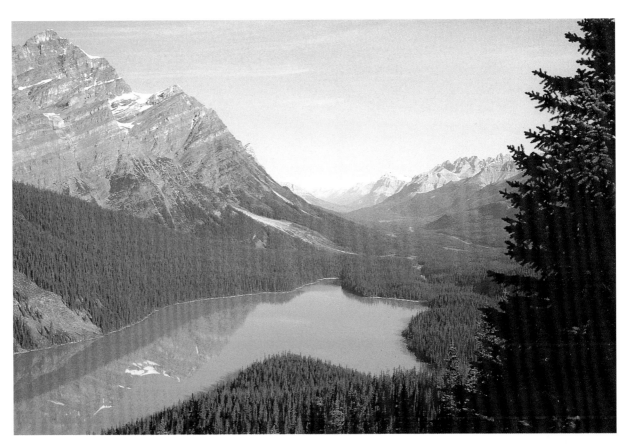

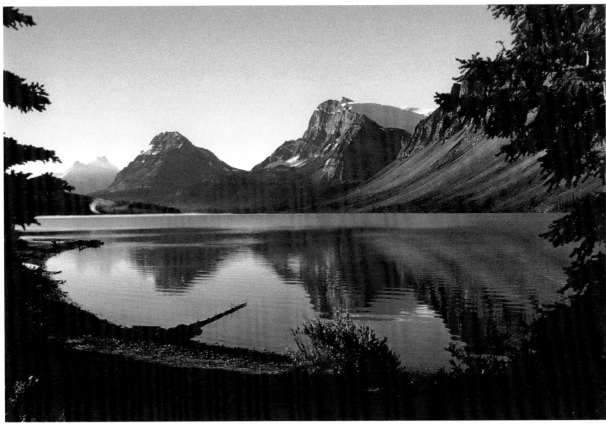

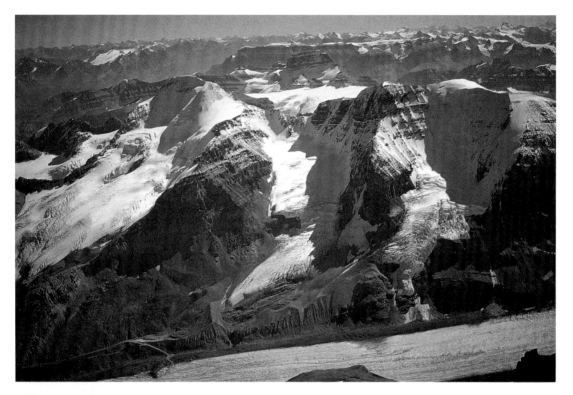

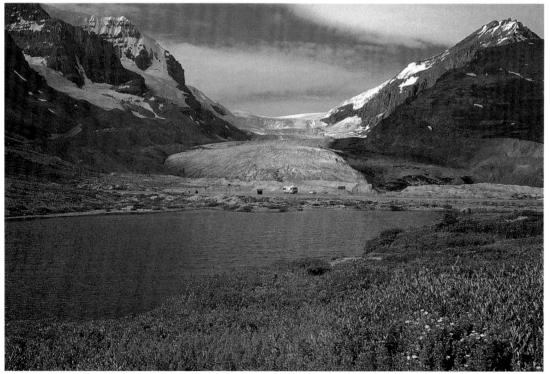

Top left:
Athabasca Glacier from Above
This aerial view gives you a sense of Athabasca Glacier being just the tip of the iceberg – or, in this case, the tip of the icefield. It's just one of many glaciers that flows from Columbia Icefield, which spreads over 337 sq km/130 sq mi of land.

Bottom left:
Athabasca Glacier
Because it comes so close to the parkway, the Athabasca is the Canadian Rockies' best-known glacier. One hundred years ago it filled the valley bottom. But now that it has receded, pink fireweed and other alpine plants can bloom here.

Opposite:
Looking south on the Icefields Parkway towards Mt. Athabasca
The now-famous Icefields Parkway, completed in the 1960's, replaced the bumpy, twisty Banff-Jasper Highway, which had been built as a relief project during the Depression. This is one of the most enchanting drives in the world.

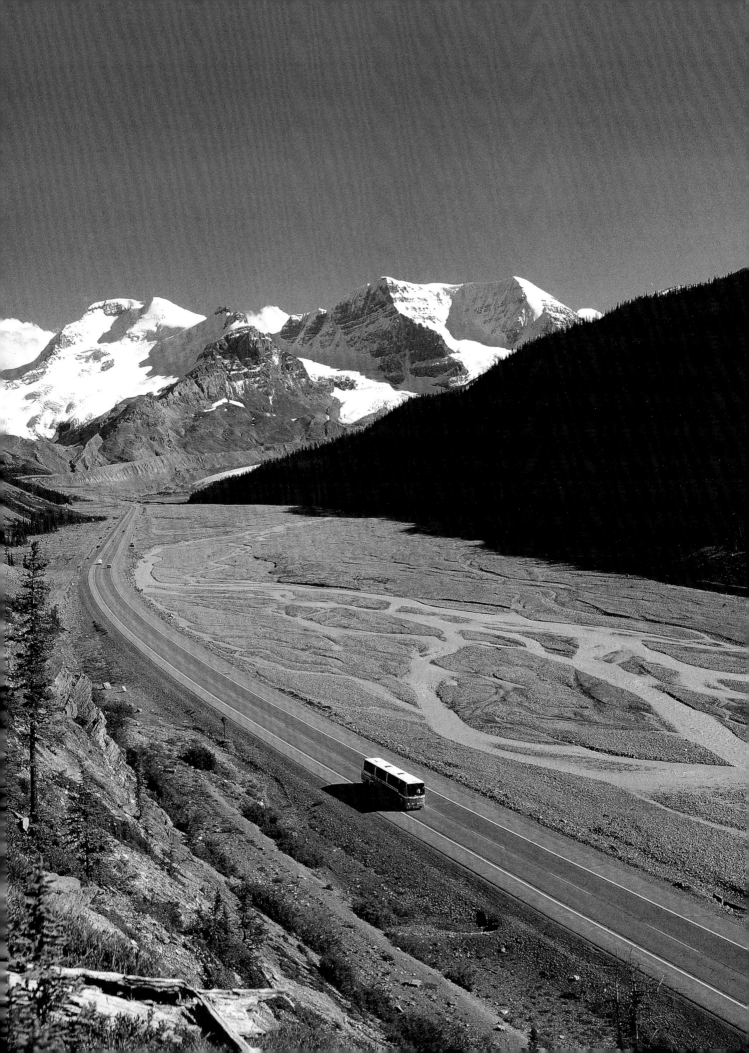

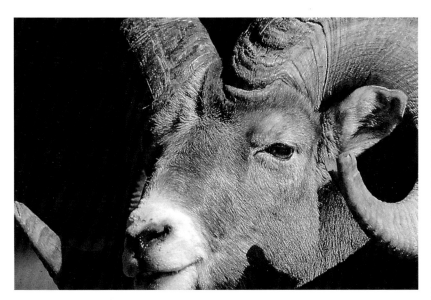

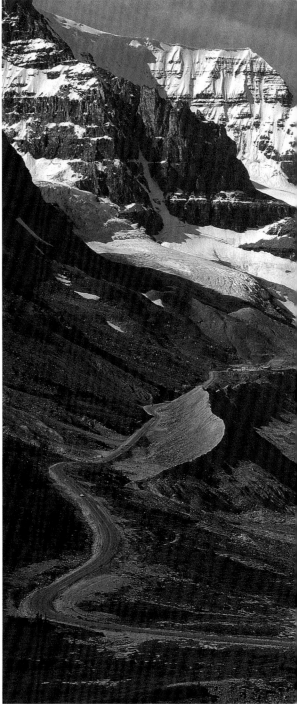

Above:
Bighorn Sheep
These cliff-dwellers are famous for the head-butting contests males hold to establish dominance. After rearing up and charging head first into each other, the pair hold still to allow inspection of one another's horns.

Opposite:
Athabasca Glacier and the Columbia Icefield Chalet
The history of the glaciers is explained at the Icefield Centre operated by Parks Canada, next to the chalet. A bit farther along you'll find the snowmobile-bus depot. That's Mt. Athabasca on the left and Mt. Kitchener on the right.

Bighorn sheep are a common sight between Athabasca Glacier and Sunwapta Falls. Please drive carefully, and do not give in to the temptation to feed these or any other animals you may encounter in the Rockies, as they can become dependent on hand-outs from humans.

The treeless swaths you'll see on the mountainsides in this area are often mistaken for ski runs, but in fact they are the product of snow avalanches. In winter and spring, park wardens periodically close the road and use explosives to trigger avalanches, in order to reduce the possibility of traffic being caught in a large slide. Near the Jonas Creek Campground, a jumbled mass of pinkish boulders covers a vast area on both sides of the road, the result of a gigantic rock slide that thundered down from the ridge to the east. Watch for roadside warning signs.

Between Sunwapta Falls and Jasper, you'll see some of the giants of the Canadian Rockies, including Mt. Edith Cavell (3363 m/11,033 ft). You can reach the base of Mt. Edith Cavell, long a favourite challenge for mountaineers, via the Athabasca Parkway (Highway 93A). The Athabasca Parkway also takes you to the roaring Athabasca Falls, where the waters of a great river tumble dramatically over a rocky ridge and through a narrow canyon. This is a cool spot in summer.

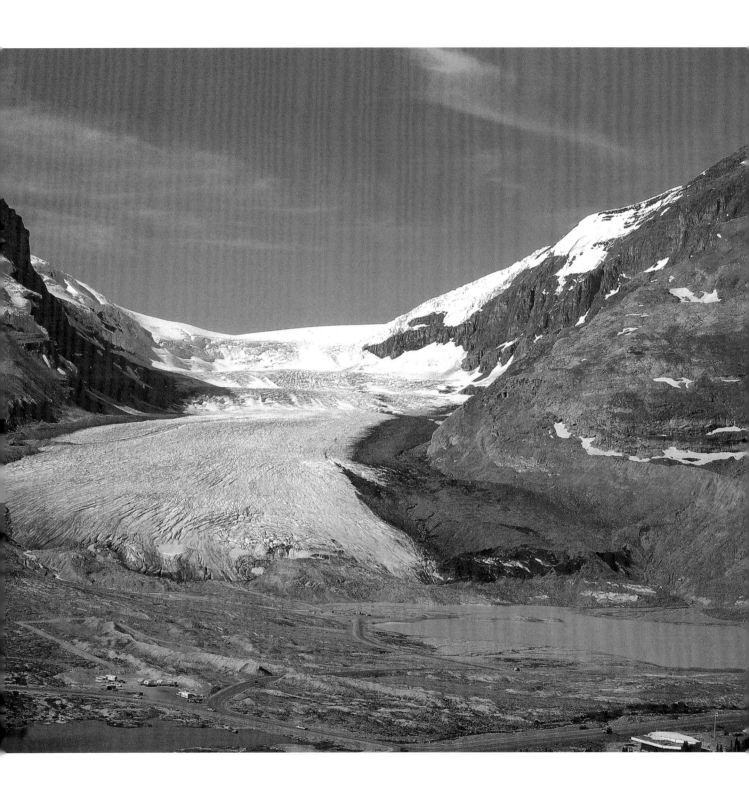

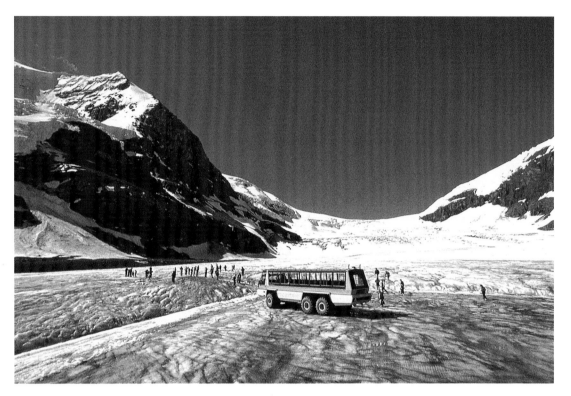

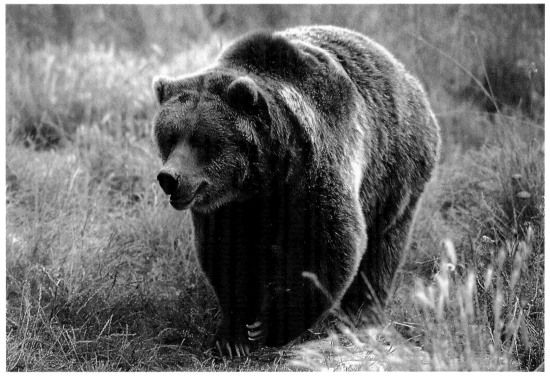

Top left:
Snowmobile on Athabasca Glacier
This is one of the most popular excursions in the Rockies. A shuttle bus takes visitors to the loading area, and from there the Snowcoach travels several kilometres along the ice to a point where visitors can take a walk on the glacier.

Bottom left:
Grizzly Bear
Please drive carefully – grizzlies are most frequently seen at roadsides between Hector Creek and Bow Pass, along the Icefields Parkway. Do not, under any circumstances, approach this or any wild animal in the Rockies.

Opposite:
Sunwapta Falls
This is where the Sunwapta River makes a sharp turn around a moraine deposited by the Columbia Glacier, and flows through a steep canyon. Downstream, a trail leads to other falls in a lower canyon.

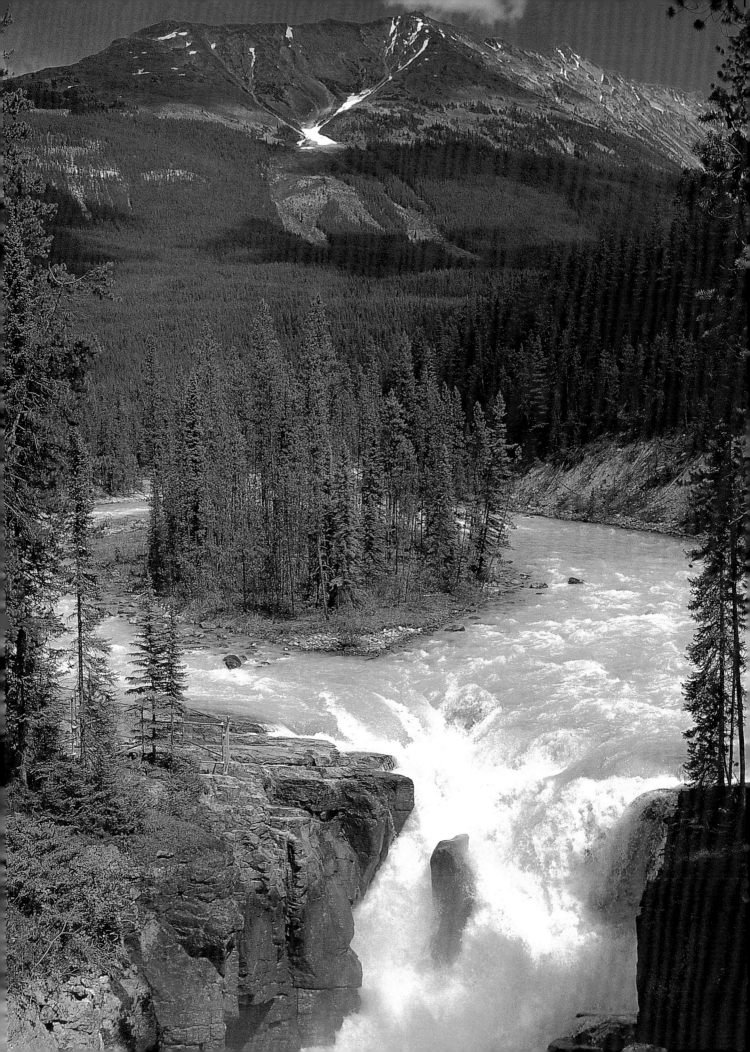

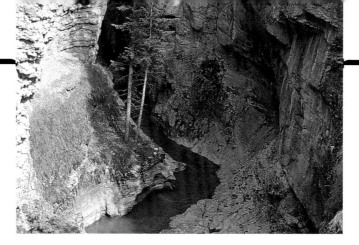

Jasper

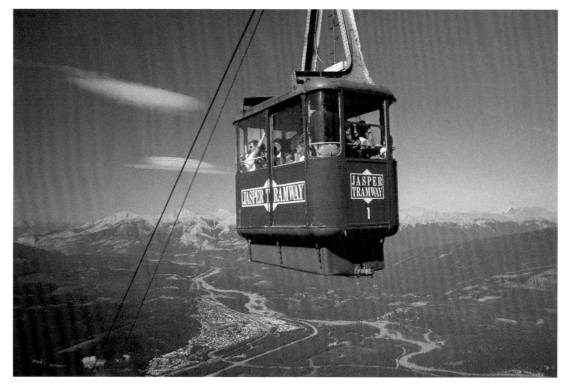

The largest of the four mountain parks is home to many of the best-known sights in the Rockies, including Mt. Robson, Maligne Lake and Spirit Island, Mt. Edith Cavell, the Miette Hot Springs and Roche Miette. This beautiful northern park is blessed with over 800 lakes and ponds, which makes it a popular destination for bird watchers, boaters, photographers and people who like to fish.

Back in the early 1800's, long before the first train whistle echoed through the Athabasca Valley, the fur-trading post presided over by Jasper Hawse of the Northwest Company was well known to the voyageurs, trappers, missionaries and local Native people. So when the Canadian government decided in

1907 to create a national park in the area, they named it after Jasper. When the railway finally made it into the valley in 1911, the town of Fitzhugh was born where the Athabasca and Miette rivers meet. Two years later its name, too, was changed to Jasper.

For an especially memorable experience, drive 6 km/3.7 mi southeast from Jasper along the Whistlers Mountain Road to the lower terminal of the Jasper Tramway. From there it will take you just seven minutes to ride to the top of the mountain in a smooth, quiet, 30-passenger cable car. At the summit there is a restaurant and a view of the surrounding mountains and valleys you'll never forget. On a clear day Mt. Robson, highest mountain in the

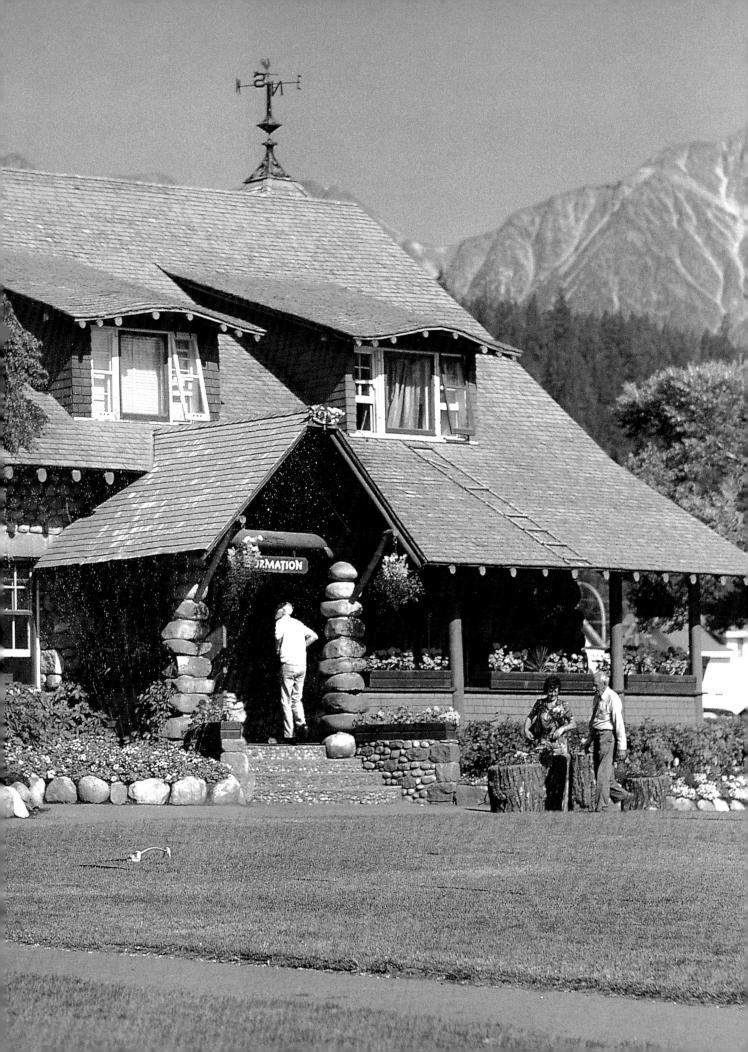

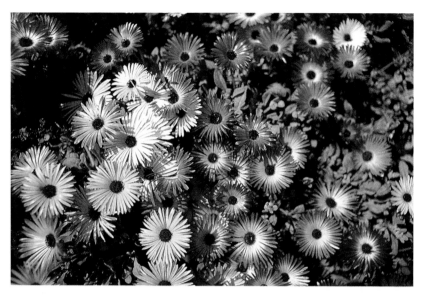

Above:
Flowers from the Gardens of the Fairmont Jasper Park Lodge

Right:
Jasper Bear
For obvious reasons, Jasper's mascot, Jasper the Bear, is very popular with young visitors. As this photo demonstrates, most kids will even stand still for a few minutes in order to have their picture taken with him.

Opposite:
Maligne Canyon
Located just outside of the town of Jasper along the road to Maligne Lake, this canyon is one of the most fascinating land forms in Jasper National Park. The canyon can be explored through a network of trails and bridges that criss-cross the top of the precipitous cliffs.

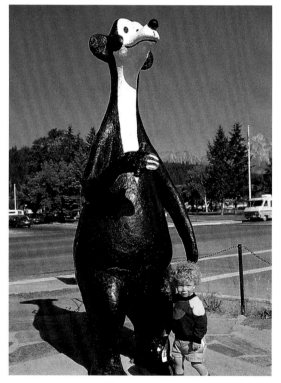

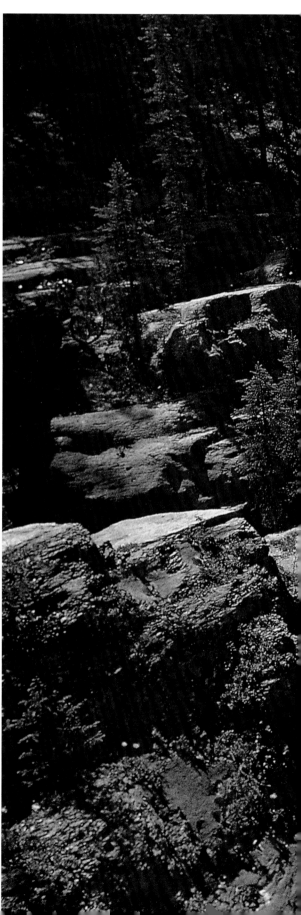

Canadian Rockies, can be seen 100 km/60 mi to the west. About 25 km closer, to the south, lies the glistening blue-white canopy of the Columbia Icefield.

Hiking is a favourite activity in the Jasper area. Countless well-groomed trails wind through the thickly wooded mountainsides, past lakes and streams where the fishing and swimming are great. Park naturalists conduct informative walking tours up in the mountains

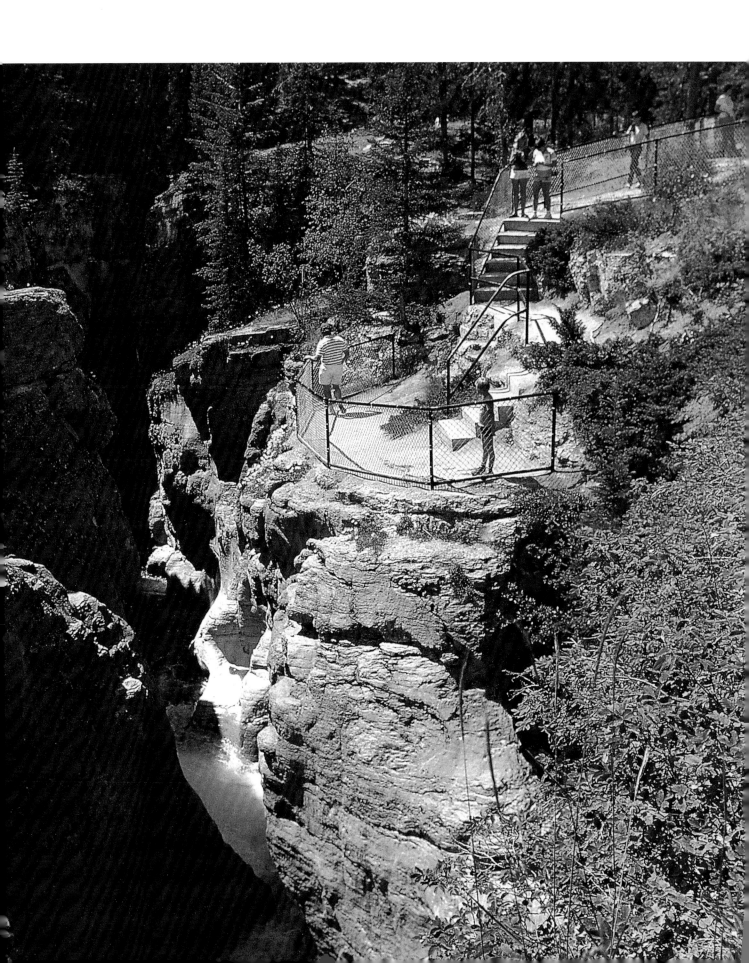

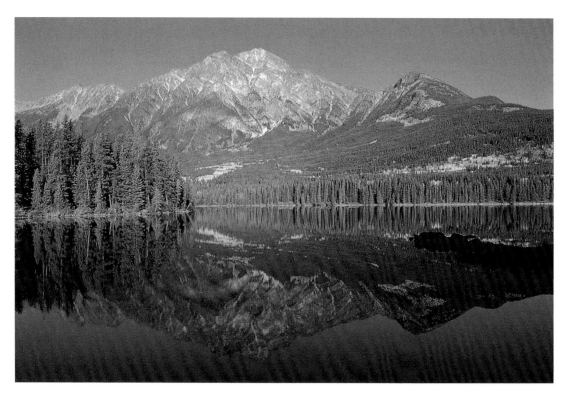

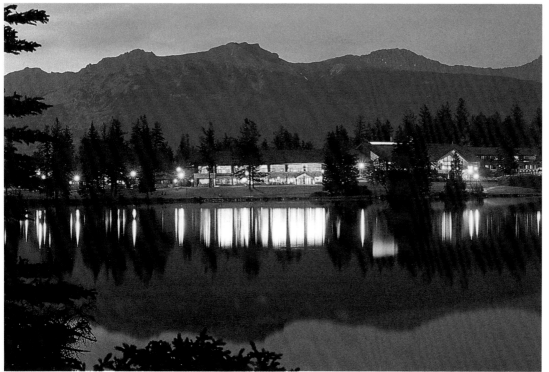

Top Left:
Pyramid Mountain and Pyramid Lake
Pyramid Lake is one of three lakes in the mountain national parks where gas-powered motor boats may be launched, so fishing and boating are very popular here. The object on the top of Pyramid Mountain is a communications tower.

Bottom left:
Fairmont Jasper Park Lodge
Thanks to its great location on the shore of Lac Beauvert, with Old Man Mountain practically in the back yard, this is a popular hotel. There is room here for 430 guests, and the Lodge is open year-round.

Opposite top:
Roche Miette on the Yellowhead Highway
Legend has it that this mountain was named after a French voyageur who climbed it and then sat smoking his pipe, with his legs dangling casually over the fearsome abyss. It's been a landmark on the Yellowhead Highway ever since.

Opposite bottom:
At the Samson Narrows, Maligne Lake
This world-famous view is the destination of the tour boats on Maligne Lake. (Also see page 42.)

and down in the valleys. For details, visit the Information Centre on Connaught Drive in Jasper.

In the winter, skiing at Marmot Basin is as good as you will find anywhere in the Rockies, whether you're an expert or a beginner. Excellent cross-country skiing can be enjoyed almost anywhere around Jasper, most notably along a network of trails on the Pyramid Bench. A lodge at Pyramid Lake offers warmth, meals and hot drinks for skiers, skaters or spectators.

The Maligne Lake Road is off Highway 16, just east of Jasper townsite, and it will take you to Maligne Canyon. This extraordinary limestone canyon is 55 m/180 ft deep in places, and yet often scarcely more than a metre wide. The

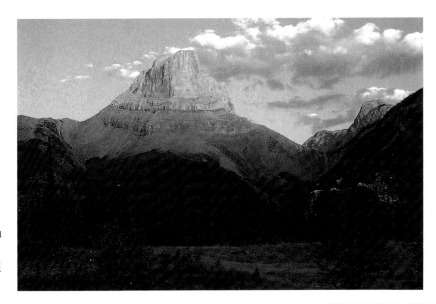

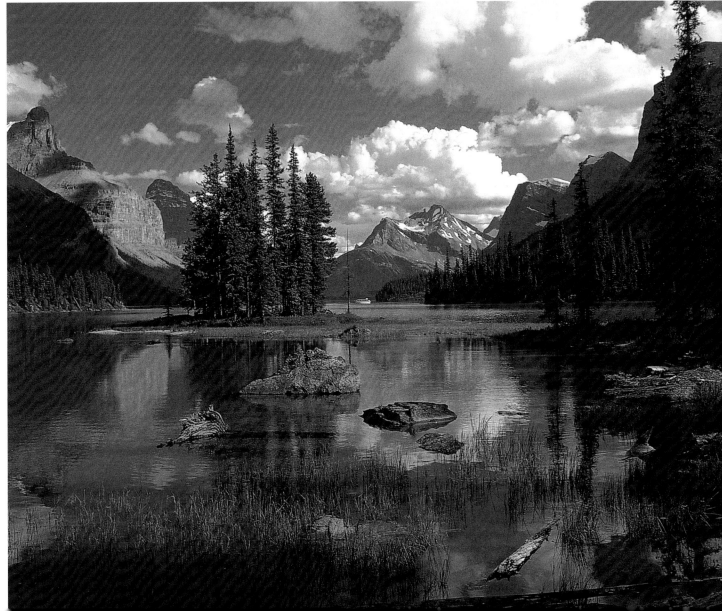

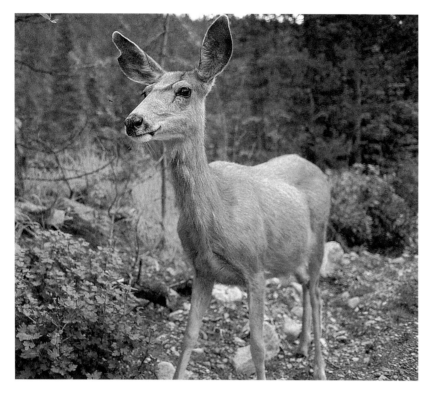

Above:
Deer, that's for sure
This looks like a white-tailed deer, but without seeing its tail it's hard to say for sure. The two kinds of deer in the Rockies are similar, but the mule deer has a narrow white tail with a black tip and the white-tailed's tail is white underneath.

Opposite:
Maligne Lake and Spirit Island
Maligne is one of the largest of the mountain lakes, stretching 14 mi/22 km through the Front Ranges near Jasper. You can see this gorgeous sight for yourself by taking the Maligne Lake boat tour or by renting a canoe or rowboat.

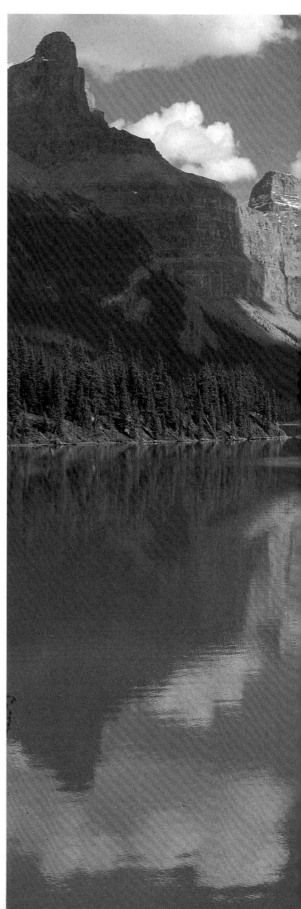

view is spectacular from any of the five bridges, which allow you to look straight down into the swirling Maligne River.

All along the forest-fringed road, there are numerous pull-outs and picnic sites with exhibits explaining the valley's geology, geography and history. Fifteen km (9 mi) along, you come to the park's most intriguing curiosity – Medicine Lake, sometimes called the 'Leaky Bathtub.' At times it looks like just another pretty mountain lake; at others it is all but dry. And yet there is no visible outlet. What happens is that when the swollen Maligne River pours into the lake, the level rises. But then, as the flow subsides in fall and winter, the water escapes through unseen holes and leaks in the lake bottom. It wanders through a network of underground streams to resurface a few kilometres downstream as a continuation of the Maligne River.

Maligne Lake, 23 km/14 mi farther up the valley, was once called 'Sore Foot Lake,' presumably by an early explorer who had his problems getting there. At 22.5 km/14 mi long and 1.6 km/1 mi across at its widest point, it is one of the largest lakes in the Rockies.

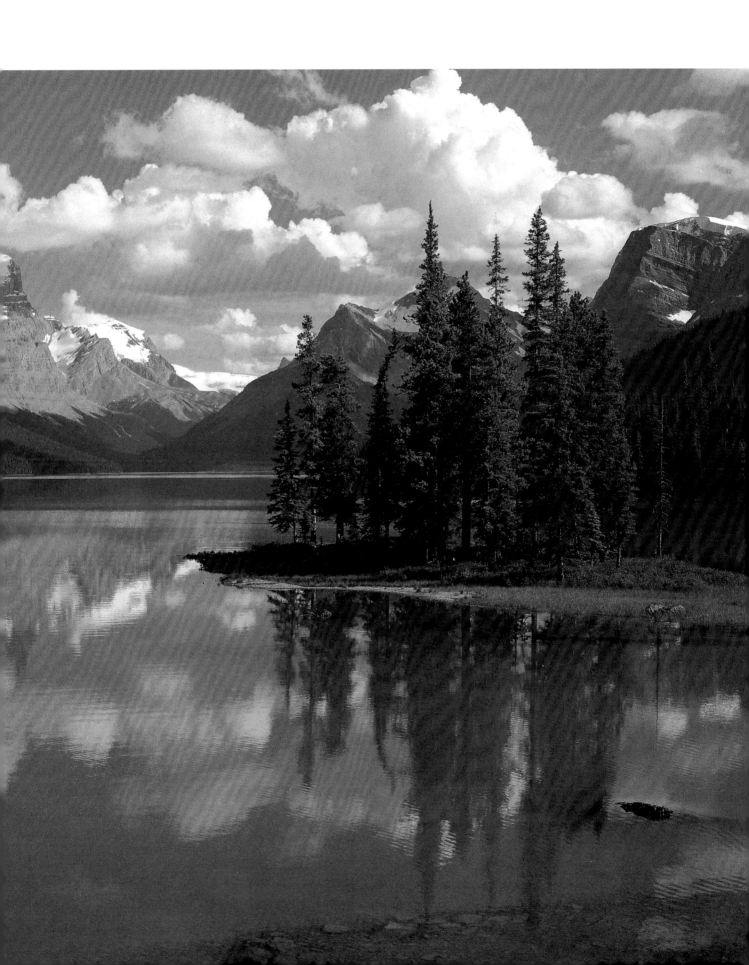

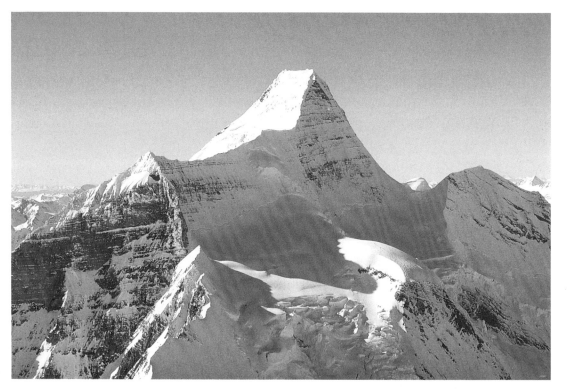

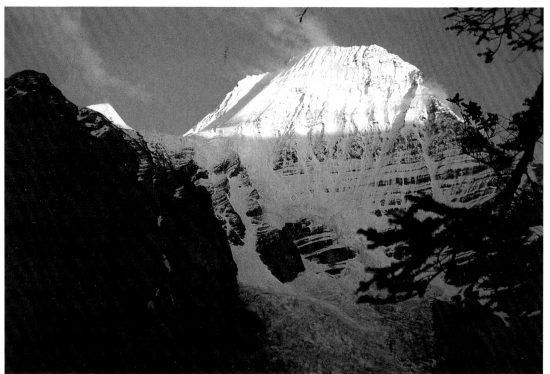

Top left:
**Mt. Robson from
the summit of
Mt. Resplendent**
The highest mountain in the
Canadian Rockies is also one
of the most ruggedly
beautiful. The first ascent is
credited to the Alpine Club
of Canada led by guide
Conrad Kain in 1913, and
Mt. Robson remains a
favourite with climbers.

Bottom left:
Mt. Robson
This is the side of Mt.
Robson you see from the
Yellowhead Highway west
of Jasper, on the way into
Mt. Robson Provincial Park.
With its 3954 m/12,972 ft
height, Robson generally
gets more than its share of
alpenglow.

Opposite:
Mt. Edith Cavell
This spectacular 3663 m/
11,033 ft peak is well worth
the side trip along Highway
93. It was named for a
heroic nurse who was shot
during WWI, and has been a
landmark for travellers in
these mountains since the
days of the fur trade.

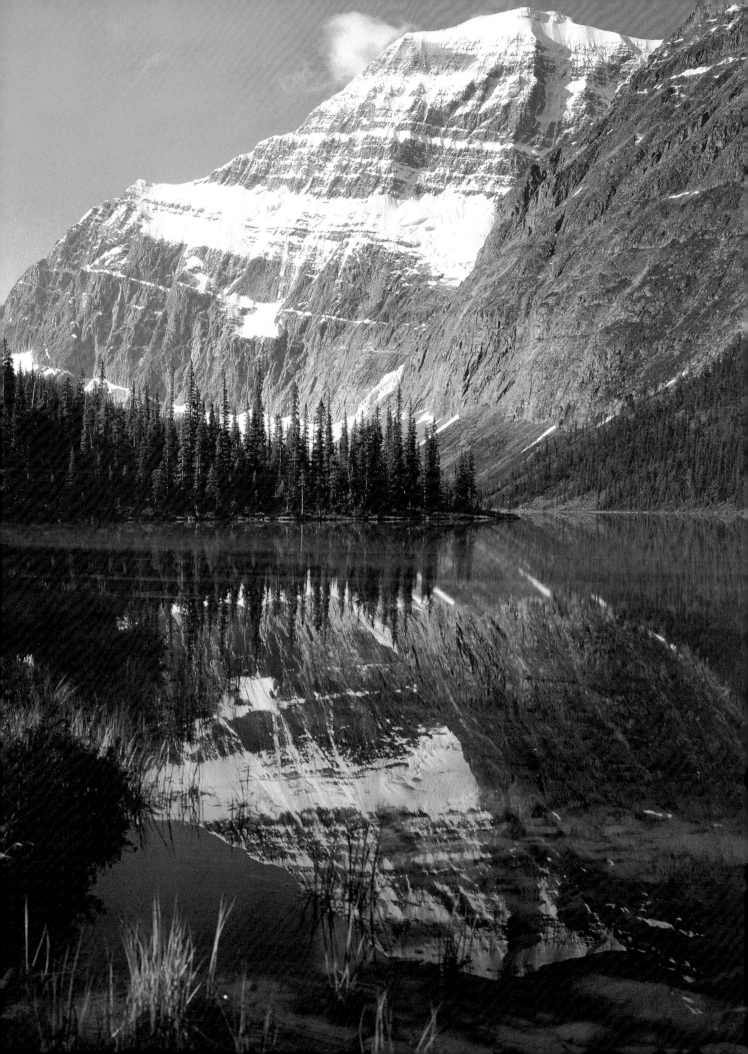

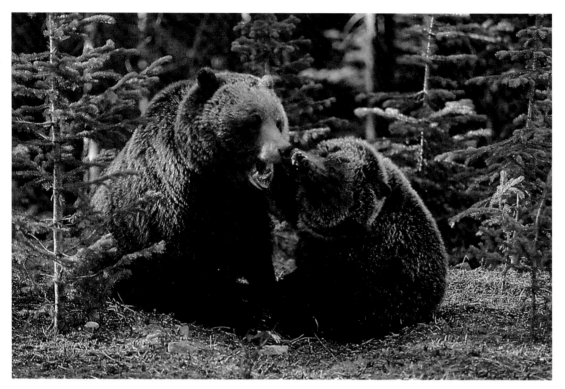

Top left:
Grizzly Bear
Despite their resemblance to teddy bears, grizzlies are the most feared of mountain mammals. They can weigh as much as 360 kg/800 lbs and can out-run a horse. For more information on bears, ask at any park information centre.

Bottom left:
Bighorn Sheep
Bighorns are often seen close to the highway where mineral licks occur near both Banff and Jasper townsites. Males sport spectacular curving horns, while females and immature males have short, pointed horns.

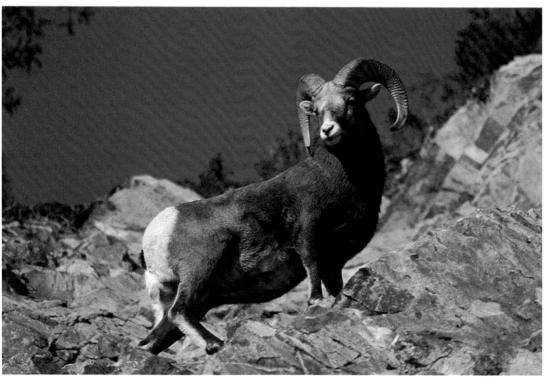

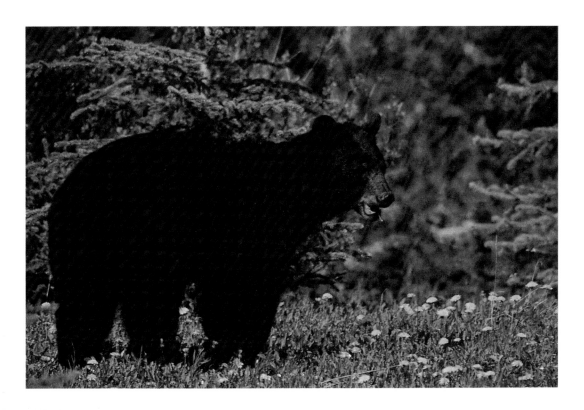

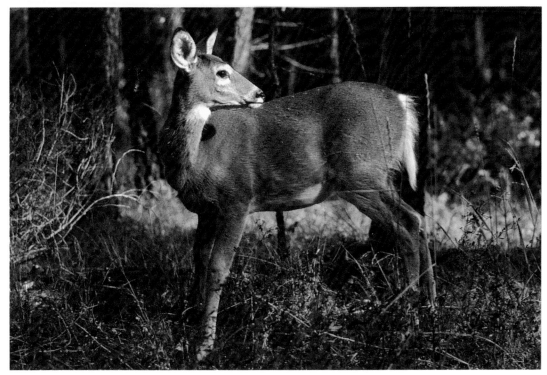

Top:
Black Bear
These animals are commonly seen in the backcountry as well as along the highways. Although not as predatory as the grizzly, these bears are equally dangerous. Their rich coat of fur ranges from black to a lighter brown colour.

Bottom:
Mule Deer
Slim, elegant and frequently mistaken for Elk, the Mule deer are commonly found **throughout the Rockies. They** run with a bounding motion, leaping high in the air to clear obstacles that might lie in their path as they speed forward.

Following page:
Twin Falls
Near the head of the Yoho Valley in Yoho National Park lies this beautiful waterfall. Legend has it that the trail crew that was building the backcountry huts for the Canadian Pacific Railway blasted the rock at the top of the cliff in order to create this twin waterfall.

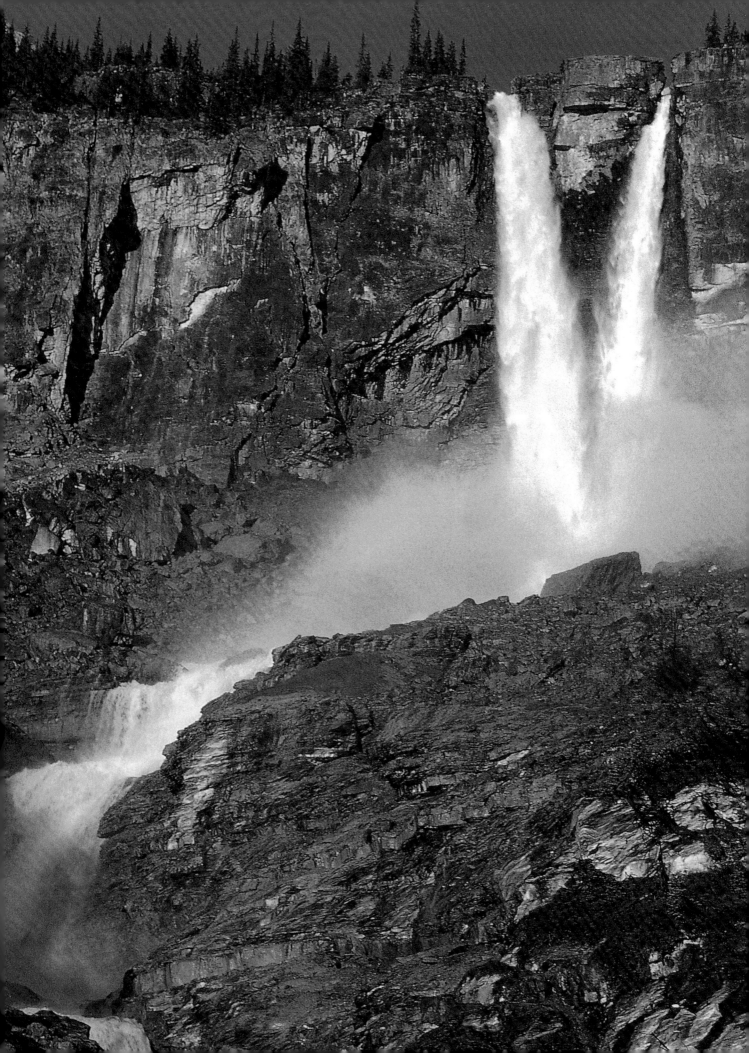